Collins
WOODLAND
TRUST

Exploring woodland

Southeast England

D0993890

101 beautiful woods to visit

Collins is an imprint of HarperCollins*Publishers* Ltd.
77–85 Fulham Palace Road
London
W6 8JB

The Collins website address is: www. collins.co.uk

10 09 08 07 06 05 04

10 9 8 7 6 5 4 3 2 1

ISBN 0 00 717547 7

First published in 2004
Text © The Woodland Trust 2004
Maps © HarperCollins*Publishers*, except for p60 © The Woodland Trust

A catalogue record for this book is available from the British Library.

Site maps produced by Belvoir Cartographics and Design
Designed by Liz Bourne
Site entries written by Sheila Ashton, researched by Sarah Underhill & Janet Watt
Edited by Graham Blight

Printed and bound by Printing Express Ltd., Hong Kong
All the paper used in this book is 100% recycled

HOW TO USE THIS BOOK

Covering a region that encompasses Kent, Surrey, Sussex, Hampshire, Isle of Wight and South London, this book is divided into three areas represented by key maps on pp18–19, 40–41, and 74-75. The tree symbols on these maps denote the location of each wood. In the pages following the key maps, the sites nearest one another are described together (wherever practical) to make planning a day out as rewarding as possible.

For each site entry the name of the nearest town/village is given, followed by road directions and the grid reference of the site entrance. The area of the site (in hectares (HA) followed by acres) is given next together with the official status of the site where appropriate. The owner, body or organisation responsible for maintaining the site is given next. Symbols are used to denote information about the site and its facilities. These are explained on p17.

Oxford

Watford

London

Southend-on-Sea

Swindon

Reading

Croydon

Gillingham

Maidstone

Basingstoke

Guildford

Royal Tunbridge Wells

Dover

Winchester

Crawley **2**

3

Southampton

Brighton

Hastings

Portsmouth

Eastbourne

1

INTRODUCTION

Woodland Trust celebrity supporter, Alistair McGowan, says:
'Can you imagine what our countryside would look like without
trees? Sound like a colourless and dreary place? Woods offer us
peace and tranquillity, inspire our imagination and creativity, and
refresh our souls. A land without trees would be a barren, cold
and impoverished place. When I want to get back in touch with
nature and escape from the hustle and bustle of my daily life, I
love to visit and explore these natural treasures. These places are
rich in wildlife and support a wide variety of animal and plant life.
This excellent series of Woodland Trust guidebooks charts some
of the most spectacular woods across the UK. You will be amazed
and inspired to discover the wide variety of cultural and ecological
history that exists in these special places. Each guide provides you
with the all the information you will ever need.'

SOUTHEAST ENGLAND

Pounding relentlessly round the M25, the nose-to-tail traffic hurtles day and night, seemingly a world away from the pastoral delights of the Kent and Surrey countryside and its remarkable array of beautiful and diverse woodlands; and yet many are but a short step from this frantic tarmac treadmill. If ever a part of Britain needed the peaceful havens of its woodlands then surely here it is paramount.

Looking at the map, the first impression of southeast England is one of a densely populated area with its associated road and rail network and yet, in spite of this, much of Kent, Sussex and Surrey, collectively known as the Weald, forms one of the most heavily wooded areas of Britain. This status has endured throughout recorded history largely because the coppice wood and larger timber were more important to the region's economy than the alternative use of the land for agriculture. In most recent history the infamous gales of 1987 did their utmost to destroy much of these woods, but even in the face of such extreme elements their vibrancy could not be quashed. Replanting and a great deal of natural regeneration has already healed most of the scars.

The splendid botanic gardens at Kew weren't spared the devastation of the gales either. However, it's a great tribute to the staff that Kew Gardens look as peerless as ever today. Not perhaps everyone's idea of woodland, but Kew does have many stands of

Sun shafts, Park Wood, p77

Alice Holt, catkins

different types of trees along with its splendid collection of individual specimen trees from around the world. This is a great place either to begin your acquaintance with trees or to broaden your knowledge; taking advantage of the 250 years of expertise, enthusiasm and commitment which have created one of the finest collections of trees and plants in the world. One of Kew's most special trees is the 'Old Lion' Ginkgo biloba - a so-called fossil tree, which is a direct descendant from the ginkgo family of 200 million years ago – once growing worldwide, but with a native range now confined to a mountainous region of southeast China. Its form has remained virtually unchanged to this day, as fossil remains found in northeast England testify. This is just one star out of many, but the importance of Kew is that this is the place to really get to grips with positively identifying trees (helpfully, they're all labelled), so that when you encounter some of the introduced or exotic species elsewhere you'll know exactly what you're looking at.

With such a large and diverse selection of woodlands to visit in the southeast it's impossible to mention most of them here, but a sampling of different types should whet the appetite for woodland adventuring.

Many of the larger open spaces with woodland in southern suburban London and northern Surrey are old parkland or commons, and all these sites have their own specific merits. Ashstead Common is most famous for its 2,000 ancient oak pollards, remnants of an old wood pasture regime. Some of the trees will be 300-400 years old and their gnarled old forms have become havens for all manner of birdlife, bats and bugs. If you're jumpy about creepy-crawlies you might not like to know that 1,000 species of beetles have been found here – 150 being internationally rare. Londoners treasure these green spaces as somewhere close at hand to walk the dog, let the kids go wild, ride bikes or horses or just sit to chill out. Wimbledon and Putney Commons offer bags of room for all this with woods predominantly oak/birch and beech/hornbeam as well as heathland and ponds all linked by a network of paths and tracks. And the bonus for your healthy exertions? Excellent Tea Rooms (by all accounts), and they're open 363 days a year!

Head east around the old South Circular, towards Dartford, to find the fascinating wood around the remains of Lesnes Abbey, near Belvedere, where archaeology, palaeontology, splendid wild flowers, a weird tree face ('Sleeping Dryad' in an old sweet chestnut), and even ring necked parakeets are some of the treats in store – you'd be hard put to get such an eclectic mix anywhere else. Incidentally, the author is slightly relieved to know that there are other people who see faces in trees too!

At Trosley Country Park, near Meopham, you'll discover some of the most splendid views from the crest of the North Downs out across the Weald of Kent, surrounded by a superb display of wild flowers so typically associated with chalk grassland and some thumping great yews, a lime loving tree which pops up frequently along the chalky uplands of the whole region. Perhaps the most glorious woodland system in east Kent is that to be found around the city of Canterbury; the north-western part being known as The Blean. At over 500 hectares (1,200+ acres) this is one of the largest broadleaved nature reserves in the whole of Britain and is

Regeneration at Ashford Hangers, p29

Fungi-clad tree stumps, Flatropers, p85

comprised of a number of different habitat types, including ancient woodland, conifer plantations, heathland and sweet chestnut coppice. It is managed by a consortium of local authorities and conservation groups. Although there are some marvellous oaks and beeches here, it's the sweet chestnut which plays the pivotal role. Chestnut coppice has been the economic mainstay of these woods, probably since Roman times, for they almost certainly introduced the tree to Britain. More recently it was cut for hop poles in the 19th and early 20th centuries, whilst smaller cleft pales were used for countless miles of Chestnut palings (or spiles). H L Edlin delivered the amazing statistic in the 1940s that, 'a skilled cleaver can make a mile of fencing, using some 25,000 pales, from an acre of chestnut coppice.' Management of these woods has been the salvation of the heath fritillary, a nationally rare butterfly, which thrives along the open rides and glades, where it finds its main food plant, cow-wheat. For bird lovers this is the place to be if you want to catch sight or sound of the elusive nightingale and nightjar.

On the Kent/Sussex border, near Goudhurst, lies Bedgebury Pinetum - one of the world's finest conifer collections. At the last count 6,241 magnificent trees, including many rare and endangered species grew amongst landscaped lakes and valleys. Established as the National Conifer Collection in 1925 it was the passion and energy of William Dallimore, a botanist/gardener who retired from Kew in 1936, which made the greatest impact at Bedgebury. For nine years he planted trees to complement the existing scheme established by Viscount Marshall Beresford, and an

Spring colour in Mens Nature Reserve, p45

ongoing sense of scale and design has culminated in a truly superb conifer experience. Whether it be enchanting wintry landscapes in the grip of sparkling hoar frost, the organised and entertaining fungus forays of autumn to seek out some of the 975 varieties identified so far, or lazy summer days relaxing by the lakes and streams and being occasionally buzzed by some of the 19 species of dragonflies, there's always something different going on here. You can even discover Kent's tallest tree - The Old Man of Kent is a whopping great Silver fir planted in 1847 and now a staggering 50 metres (163 feet) high.

Once upon a time in Sussex there was a forest where a small boy and his animal friends had marvellous adventures, and eventually their story was told to the whole world. Ashdown Forest might not look like the wooded forest of the story books, for it is forest in the legal sense – a preserve where the king (or landowner) would hunt his deer at his leisure. Ironically it was the excessive numbers of deer plus the over grazing of livestock by the commoners which denuded much of Ashdown of its trees. Certainly there must once have been respectable amounts of coppice woodland here since the forest was at the hub of a vibrant iron industry from the Roman occupation through to the end of the 18th century, and copious quantities of wood were needed to make the charcoal to fire the furnaces to smelt the iron ore. All that's left today is plenty of colonizing birch, some good stands of pine and an abundance of heathland (one of Britain's fastest disappearing habitats). The big attraction of Ashdown for many is the A A Milne association of

Christopher Robin and his animal pets; and it is, after all, great fun to visit The Enchanted Place (Gill's Lap) or play Pooh Sticks from the actual bridge that E H Shepherd drew.

Not far from Uckfield a different kind of woodland story unfolds, and not only one from which pleasure can be taken, but also a hugely informative experience encompassing the socio-economic value of woodlands both now and in the past. Wilderness Wood is managed by its resident owners as a working wood; growing sweet chestnut, pine and beech, which are harvested and converted into wood products on site. In addition every effort has been made to work in close harmony with the wildlife as well as providing educational and recreational facilities for visitors. There are frequent special events and demonstrations throughout the year, and just before Christmas you can even go and cut or dig your very own Christmas tree. The all round excellence of this woodland and the Yarrow family who run it so enthusiastically has led to several prestigious awards in recent years.

In stark contrast to the active management at Wilderness it's interesting to take stock of a real wilderness and the way that lack of management shapes woodland. Near Petworth is an ancient common, largely composed of wood-pasture, called The Mens. Grazing of livestock ceased here a long time ago, so that much of the old pasture slowly evolved into woodland. Amongst the younger woodland trees huge old oak pollards and towering beeches interspersed by medieval wood banks and flower rich meadows form a delicious tract of landscape history which has

Fantastic old trees, Moat Wood, p73

survived almost unchanged for centuries. The name may seem strange, but it apparently derives from the Anglo-Saxon 'ge-maennes', meaning 'common land'. This is a wonderful untamed space which will hopefully stay this way in the safe hands of Sussex Wildlife Trust.

The rich tapestry of our nation's history is well woven into so many of the southeastern woodlands, manifesting in all kinds of evidence of ownership, occupation and woodmanship. Take Moat Wood, for example, near East Hoathly, containing (obviously) a moat. Research has revealed that this probably dates from the 13th century and that a homestead with several associated farm buildings once stood upon the island it surrounds; the moat itself being more a status symbol than a defence, and quite handy as a ready source of fresh fish for the table. The woodland at Oldbury Hill (near Sevenoaks) is topped by a massive Iron Age hill fort, whilst at Joydens Wood (near Dartford) there are remains of two Iron Age roundhouses and an ancient bank and ditch (Faesten Dic) strikes through the wood. Wherever you go there are signs of the past if you can only tune into them. Watch for ancient drove roads, iron workings, charcoal hearths, saw-pits, hammer ponds and quarries. If you see things you don't understand, try and find out more; for when you understand the structure and evolution of woodland it brings a whole new dimension to your visits.

Japanese larch cones, Alice Holt, p26

Step back through history on Oldbury Hill, p82

Sometimes a woodland experience can be one of awesome proportions, and perhaps few more so than a remarkable place set in the chalk downs a little way north of Chichester. If you can, go to Kingley Vale early on a misty morning, before the rest of the world is up and about. Tread cautiously into the dark depths of this ancient yew wood, keeping a watchful eye on the massive arachnoid trees, many at least 500 years old, as they crouch menacingly in the gloom. The whole place engenders a sense of edgy wonder; a sense of being watched; a sense of smallness and insignificance. Did that one just move? If you're of a nervous disposition take a friend. The site is generally considered to be the best of its type in Europe and in 1952 it became one of Britain's first designated National Nature Reserves. In the early 20th century W.H. Hudson was moved to write: 'One has here the sensation of being in a vast cathedral: not like that of Chichester, but older and infinitely vaster, fuller of light and gloom and mystery, and more wonderful in its associations.'

It mustn't be forgotten that just across the Solent lies the Isle of Wight, with many interesting woodlands and some of Britain's slippiest and slidiest landscape in its south coast landslips, well worth a visit if you want to see trees literally hanging in there. Parkhurst Forest is a pleasant mixture of broadleaves and conifers and one of the largest tracts of woodland on the island, tracing its roots back to the Domesday Book. America Wood, near Shanklin, which is principally oak, chestnut and sycamore, is probably just

Bracket fungus,
Guestling Wood,
p84

as old and yet its name only dates from the 1770s (prior to that it was called Little Castle Wood). Tradition has it that oak from the wood was used to build warships sent out to fight in the American War of Independence. This brings to the fore yet another intriguing aspect of woods – unravelling the meanings behind their names. While on the Island don't forget to keep a watchful eye out for red squirrels, as this is one of their last strongholds in southern England.

Instead of ferrying back to the racket of city life in Portsmouth or Southampton take the more peaceful connection from Yarmouth to Lymington and explore the New Forest, enjoying a little of its 26,500 hectares (65,500 acres) of woodland of different types and sizes, open heath, ponds, streams, bogs and grassland. This is a huge location, and not only due to its size, but also because of its rich biodiversity, a landscape little changed in 1,500 years and its superlative amenity value. The Court of Verderers looks after the interests of the commoners of the forest in conjunction with the Forestry Commission who attend to the woodland management. The New Forest is set to become a

Autumn floor in
Guestling, p84

Detail of tree trunks, Ashford Hangers, p29

National Park, which should help to assure its future.

Beech, and splendid specimens at that, may be a well known feature of the New Forest (although the grey squirrels are doing their level best to change that), but to the north-east are the famous Hampshire beech hangers where dramatic chalky scarps are clad in towering swathes of trees; and none of these more famed than Selborne Hanger. The village, along with its surrounding countryside has found immortality since the late 18th century when one of Britain's most celebrated naturalist/diarists, Rev. Gilbert White, published his 'Natural History of Selborne', recording the minutest detail of the natural world he observed around his Hampshire home. Even today a visit to Selborne is redolent of White's accounts and it is an evocative perambulation up through the hanger along his zig-zag path. Sadly the ancient yew tree sentinel in front of Selborne church blew down in the 1990 gales, and although the massive bole was gently levered back into the ground, with the hopes of regeneration, it still perished. Nearby Binswood is an ancient common, once part of the Wolmer Forest, still grazed by commoners' stock and characterised by craggy old oak and beech pollards as well as the many areas of flower rich grassland. These peaceful corners of Hampshire seem a million miles from the hustle and bustle of London, but there are numerous woodland treats to be discovered a short way out of the metropolis.

Box Hill, near Dorking, is a splendid example of a woodland type now reduced to a handful of such sites nationally. Box is a native evergreen more usually associated with historic parterres or the topiaric excesses of formal gardens, but here it sprawls most informally hither and yon across the hill. Box wood was once a supremely valuable commodity prized by wood engravers for making blocks, but this market declined significantly after the 19th century in the face of technological improvements in commercial printing. There are still many artist wood engravers today who use the wood, but nothing approaching the same sort of scale. It has been estimated that more than a million people visit Box Hill every year and on a hot summer's day that seems a believable statistic, but try a visit 'off peak' and enjoy a good burrow around in the mysterious box groves, and discover some fine old yews, some goodly beeches and one of the lesser known rarities on the lower slopes, large-leaved lime.

The view from Box Hill is pretty fine, but for perhaps the most impressive view in the whole of Surrey head over to the other side of Dorking to Leith Hill. From the top of the tower on Leith Hill, built in 1765, you stand 317 metres (1,040 feet) above sea level, and on a clear day you'll see across 13 counties. It's hard to believe that the 1987 gales wreaked such devastation here, throughout the Wealden landscape laid before you, and yet it's equally reassuring to realise how good nature is at setting herself to rights. Trees in particular are tenacious and resilient in the face of adversity and no matter what the elements (and sometimes us as well) do to them they will be around for a few more million years yet. So, study this book, realise what a treasure house of woodland is waiting for you in southeast England, and get out there and enjoy it.

Archie Miles

Quick Reference

Symbols used to denote information about each site and the facilities to be found there.

Type of wood
- ⬛ Mainly broadleaved woodland
- ⬛ Mainly coniferous woodland
- ⬛ Mixed woodland

Car Park
- ℗ Parking on site
- ℗ Parking nearby
- ⬛ Parking difficult to find

Status
AONB Area of Outstanding Natural Beauty
SSSI Site of Special Scientific Interest

Site Facilities
- ⬛ Sign at entry
- ⬛ Information board
- ♿ One or more paths suitable for wheelchair users
- ⬛ Dogs allowed under supervision
- ⬛ Waymarked trail
- ⬛ Toilet
- ⬛ Picnic area
- £ Entrance/car park charge
- ⬛ Refreshments on site

Mysterious gnarled images,
Stansted Forest, p31

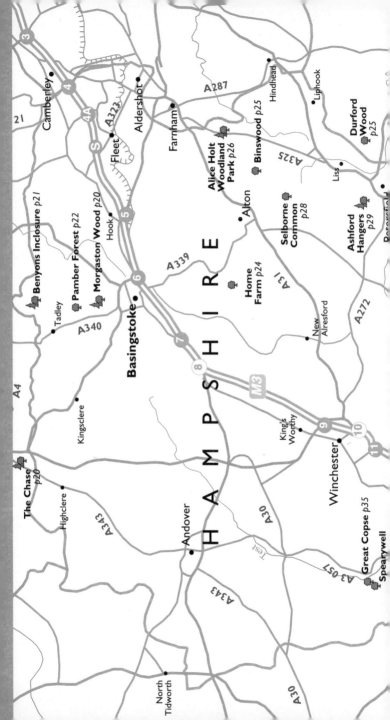

3

Camberley

4

4A

A323

Aldershot

A287

Hindhead

Liphook

Durford Wood p25

21

Fleet

Farnham

Binswood p25

Liss

5

Alice Holt Woodland Park p26

Benyons Inclosure p21

Pamber Forest p22

Morgaston Wood p20

Hook

A339

Selborne Common p28

Ashford Hangers p29

Alton

Tadley

A340

6

Home Farm p24

A31

A272

Basingstoke

New Alresford

A4

Kingsclere

7

H A M P S H I R E

8

M3

King's Worthy

9

10

11

The Chase p20

Highclere

A343

Andover

A30

Winchester

Test

Great Copse p35

A3057

Spearywell

A343

North Tidworth

A30

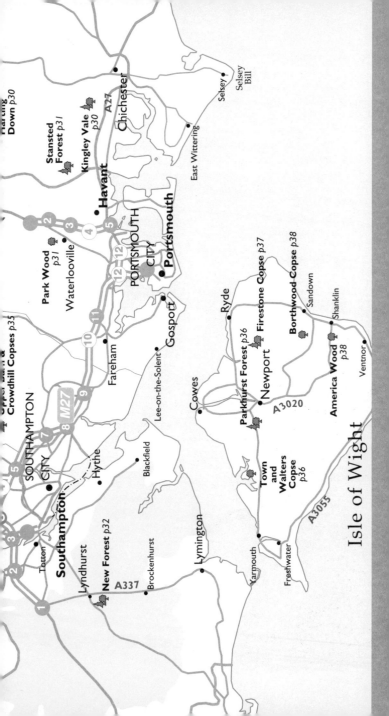

Harting
Down p30

Stansted
Forest p31

Kingley Vale
p30

A27

Chichester

Selsey

Selsey
Bill

Park Wood
p31

Waterlooville

Havant

East Wittering

2

3

4

5

12—12

PORTSMOUTH
CITY

Portsmouth

11

Firestone Copse p37

Borthwood Copse p38

10

Gosport

Ryde

Sandown

SOUTHAMPTON
CITY

Upper Barn &
Crowdhill Copses p35

M27

9

Fareham

Parkhurst Forest p36

Newport

America Wood
p38

Shanklin

8

7

Lee-on-the-Solent

Cowes

A3020

Ventnor

Hythe

5

Blackfield

Town
and
Walters
Copse
p36

Southampton

Totton

Lyndhurst

New Forest p32

Brockenhurst

A337

Lymington

Yarmouth

Freshwater

A3055

1

2

3

Isle of Wight

The Chase

Broadlayings, Woolton Hill.
5km (3 miles) southwest of Newbury
on the A343. Go through Broadlaying,
following brown signs to Rampant Cat
public house. Go past the pub and the
wood is on the right, but keep going
and turn right at T-junction, signposted
to Newbury. Car park is on right.
(SU442630)
56HA (138ACRES)
The National Trust

Easy on the eye – and the legs
– The Chase is a wood packed
with variety – conifers and
broadleaves, young and mature

The Chase

trees, dry open areas and wet
woodland with formal and
informal paths.

Although there is no map or
waymarked trail there is a clear
path and it is not too difficult
to find your way around.

Along the way you
encounter all manner of trees
from conifers to sweet
chestnut. Follow a gravel track
to the edge of open meadow
where stands a magnificent
spreading beech – take a seat
and enjoy the view.

Away from the main path
are grassy, sunny glades – great
for butterflies during spring
and summer.

A huge pond with a weir and
central island stands in the
wood's northeast corner. The
scene then changes gradually
from open water through marshy,
boggy areas to alder and
willow woodland – wonderful
for flora and fauna.

Morgaston Wood

Sherborne St John
6.5km (4 miles) north of Basingstoke.
Take the A340 Aldermaston Road out
of Basingstoke. Turn right into
Morgaston Road. Roadside parking and
main National Trust car park.
(SU625572)
63HA (156ACRES)
The National Trust

Morgaston Wood provides the perfect complement to a tour of the National Trust's neighbouring Vyne Estate.

Change and contrast are key features of the wood which is quite a mixture of woodland species, from larch, pine, poplar and hazel to birch, alder, oak and sycamore. Entered from the roadside parking area on Morgaston Road, you quickly encounter two lovely large beech and oak trees.

Here and there are signs of coppicing, elsewhere there are tall dark conifers including a stand planted on what looks like an old pond.

The contrast between the rich mix of plants and shrubs beneath the broadleaves stands out against the bare ground supporting the conifers.

Other points of interest include a stream which runs along the wood's southern edge and the occasional seat for rest and reflection.

There is a good variety of paths and part of the wood has a concrete track, which should suit wheelchair users.

Benyons Inclosure

Mortimer West End, Silchester
The wood is on the south side of Welshman's road, the road from Mortimer going west towards Heath End, immediately after Mortimer West End. Roadside parking. (SU625640)

190HA (470ACRES)
The Englefield Estate

While this privately owned woodland is commercially managed for timber, there is also an emphasis on conservation and public access.

Scots pine is the main species in this largely coniferous plantation but you will find broadleaved trees growing naturally along the edges of the wide rides.

Explore the eastern edge of the wood to discover a large, attractive lake with water lilies. Look for signs of a Roman road which runs northwest to southeast across the southern section and, nearby, the site of an old fort.

There is plenty to enjoy in this area. A couple of miles away is the Roman site of Silchester and continue south again to visit the ancient woodland of Pamber Forest (see next page) – a wonderful opportunity to compare and contrast two distinctly different woodland characters.

The wood provides easy walking and is enjoyed by local people.

Pamber Forest

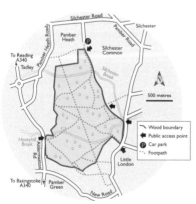

Tadley

Off A340 Basingstoke/Tadley road. Turn east at Pamber Green towards Bramley, then north to Little London and Silchester. At end of Little London, entrance is on left, opposite end of Frog Lane. (SU625605)

191HA (472ACRES) SSSI

Hampshire Wildlife Trust

Once part of the huge Royal Forest of Windsor, Pamber Forest is a well-managed and maintained ancient woodland that provides a real feeling of peace.

A walk through Pamber leads visitors through a host of habitats, each supporting its own distinct range of wildlife. The presence of roe deer explains why high fencing has been placed around certain areas to protect the young growth on freshly coppiced trees.

The scenery changes from dry open heathland through to dense hazel and sweet chestnut coppice, wood pasture, rich willow and alder-lined stream valleys.

On the woodland floor, particularly in the valleys, orchids can be seen growing alongside wild daffodils, primroses, violets, Solomon's seal and star of Bethlehem.

Some lovely big oaks, birch and hundreds of the scarce wild service tree make up the woodland, intersected by numerous wide sunlit rides edged with butterfly-attracting plants.

More than 40 butterfly species have been recorded but king of all must be the purple emperor which descends briefly from the canopy in early July. Other rare butterflies include the small pearl-bordered fritillary which can be seen in June and the silver-washed fritillary and white admiral can be glimpsed in the glades during July and August.

The wildlife interest doesn't stop there. The ponds in summer are frenetic with darting dragonflies, several species of bat have been spotted on the wing at twilight and birdlife includes woodcock, three species of woodpecker and a variety of warblers. In spring look for grass snakes, slow worms, adders and lizards.

Pamber used to provide timber for local crafts and industries and the traditional management of coppicing still continues. The forest today is managed both for conservation and visitors who enjoy an extensive network of paths throughout the reserve, including circular trails from the main entrances.

You may also like to visit adjacent Silchester Common and view the remains of the Roman town of Calleva, meaning 'Woodland Town'. Pamber is all that survives of the ancient woodland that once surrounded the site. An exploration of the 1.5 miles of walls and a viewing of the amphitheatre clearly demonstrates this was once a thriving place.

Home Farm

Burkham, Bentworth

Approx 16km (10 miles) on the A339
south of Basingstoke. On left hand side
take a right turn on a bend signposted
Bradley and Burkham. Right at the
T-junction then sharp left after half a
mile. (SU655420)
137HA (340ACRES)
The Woodland Trust

Home Farm is set in a rolling
landscape mosaic of farmland,
woodland and hedgerows.

Visitors can witness a wood at
different stages of development.
Begin by wandering through
areas of ancient and maturing
woodland before emerging into
more open spaces where young
trees are beginning to establish.

There is also an area of
grassland creation.

The number and range of
bird species visiting and
nesting has increased in recent
years. A number of owl and
kestrel boxes were installed in
2000, and barn owls are
regularly seen today.

A network of surrounding
small woods and hedgerows
virtually link Home Farm to
oak woodland at Preston Oak
Hills and Herriard Common, a
planted conifer wood. These
connect with other woods of
substantial size in the area which
provide important corridors for
wildlife.

An extensive ride network,
open spaces, a car park and
information boards all add to
the public enjoyment of this site.

Binswood

Binswood

East Worldham

A31 to Alton. From Alton take B3004
through East Worldham, 3km (2 miles)
take a right turn into a minor road (only
signpost is for a bridleway). 250 metres,
park at entrance to wood. (SU767377)

61HA (151ACRES) SSSI

The Woodland Trust

Binswood is a random mosaic
of grassland and woodland that
is literally enveloped in the past.

Indeed the site is practically
surrounded by historic boundary
banks and hedges that provide
intriguing pointers to its
history. The common was once
part of Wolmer Forest, a royal
hunting forest, and had a close
association with the medieval
deer park of Worldham.

This is one of just a few
remaining lowland woodland
pastures outside the New Forest
still sustained by traditional
grazing.

As a result it provides a
glimpse of the landscape as it
may well have looked in
medieval times, a combination
of species-rich ancient
woodland, unimproved
grassland, scrub and ancient
oaks and beech trees.

One of the most striking
features is the array of fungi
and lichens that cling to the
veteran trees.

Durford Wood

Rogate

From the Jolly Drovers public house on
the B2070 (the old A3), head east
towards Rogate. Car park is 400m (0.25
mile) on the right. (SU799260)

26HA (64ACRES) AONB

The National Trust

Here is a wood within a wood.
Surrounded by wooded common
– principally a plantation of Scots
pine, Durford is an oasis of
deciduous trees.

One hundred and fifty years
ago the area would have looked
quite different. The site was
probably part of an extensive
heath but was then planted with
oak and coppiced to provide
charcoal for the iron industry.

No longer coppiced, the
distinctively shaped trees have
developed into a fine example of
sessile oak woodland which
supports a variety of birds and
insects. There is plenty of year-
round interest starting with wood
anemones and bluebells in spring
through to heather glades in late
summer and good autumn colour.

The National Trust is creating
glades and wide tracks to
ensure the heathland character
is not lost.

Whilst in the area you may
also like to visit nearby
Forestry Commission sites at
Combe Hill and Tullecombe.

Alice Holt Woodland Park

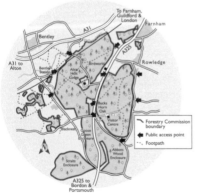

Farnham

Follow the A325 south from Farnham
for 6.5km (4 miles). Turn left at
crossroads by the Halfway House (PH).
Car park is 400m (0.25 mile) on the left.
(SU810415)

248HA (620ACRES)

Forestry Commission

Pack a picnic and spend a day in Alice Holt Woodland Park – the perfect place for families to enjoy a quiet walk, take a cycle ride, learn about wildlife or simply let off steam.

The site is managed not only for timber production but has a strong emphasis on visitor enjoyment and keeping resident wildlife happy – this is truly a site with something for everyone.

The park features a wide range of amenities including a visitor centre with a shop, classroom, play areas, cycle hire, picnic areas and barbecue sites. There is also a bridlepath and a large pond within the woods.

The woodland, a mix of broadleaves and conifers, has a good collection of old and young trees and the combination of wide tracks and narrow paths beneath the closed canopy creates an interesting blend of light and shade.

Well interpreted, the site also features a habitat trail with large wooden play sculptures to discover – among them an owl, woodpecker, bat and dragonfly. You are just as likely to spy more animated wildlife, for the woods are alive with birds and butterflies, including the purple emperor which favours the tall oaks.

On the other side of the A325 is a quieter, ancient woodland with its own parking, picnic areas, informal trails and a network of paths for those keen on exploring.

This ancient forest is famous for its oaks which once supplied timber for the navy. More recently, oaks from Alice Holt were used to create the replica of Shakespeare's Globe Theatre in London.

The woodland boasts other historical links – during Roman times the site was important for pottery and Norman kings transformed it into a royal hunting forest.

The Hangers

Some of Hampshire's most beautiful, vibrant countryside awaits on the ancient and intimate swathes of steep wooded hillside known as the Hangers.

Characterised by the beech and yew of their steepest slopes, the Hangers are of international importance for their ecology. Beneath the heavy shade of beech and yew few plants survive but out in the open glades and grassy clearings a delightful variety of wild flowers includes wood spurge, purple orchid, foxglove, tutsan and deadly nightshade. Rare and unusual species characteristic of the Hangers include sword leaved helleborines and herb paris. Various fungi, insects, rare molluscs and nesting birds also thrive here along with roe deer, badgers and foxes.

Surviving downland areas on the slopes boast a wealth of flora including thyme, rock rose, cowslip and eyebright. Discover the best of them at Wheatham Hill and Shoulder of Mutton Hill.

Hampshire County Council has devised a 21-mile linear path running south from Alton Railway Station through the Hangers to the South Downs at Queen Elizabeth Country Park.

Selborne Common

Alton

6.5km (4 miles) south of Alton between Selborne and Newton Valence, west of B3006. Zig-zag path and woods are a short walk from car park in village (adjacent to the Selborne Arms). (SU742335)

98HA (242ACRES) AONB SSSI

The National Trust

Selborne

One of Hampshire's renowned hangers (or wooded slopes) can be found near the village of Selborne.

Hangers such as this are acclaimed as some of the richest woodland on English chalk and Selborne's is particularly important for helleborines as well as hellebores.

Beautiful beech trees – providing light in spring and colour in autumn – dominate the hanger but there is lots more to discover. Half the common is made up of relict wood pasture with ancient beech pollards. This area is of great ecological and landscape importance. In the area known as High Wood look for evidence of former coppicing.

A zig-zag path leads up the steep hill to the common. At the top is a wishing stone with a seat nearby and from here you can enjoy excellent views over the village and surrounding countryside.

The common is served by paths to Newton Valence and Selborne village.

Ashford Hangers

Petersfield

North from Petersfield to Steep, through village and right at bottom of hill by cottage into Ashford Lane. Reserve entrance along lane, on left.
(SU730265)
147HA (363ACRES) AONB SSSI

Hampshire County Council

Queen Elizabeth Country Park

Petersfield

Signed on A3, just south of Petersfield.
(SU717182)
566HA (1,400ACRES) AONB SSSI
Forestry Commission/Hampshire County Council

Dominated by the three hills of Butser, War Down and Holt Down, the park combines beautiful woodland, good visitor and children's facilities and recreation opportunities. Part of the forest has been designated a Scheduled Ancient Monument due to its Iron Age and Roman remains.

Graded waymarked trails through beautiful, scenic beech woods and areas of established conifer plantation offer a range of opportunities for a woodland stroll or a horse or bike ride. West of the A3 is Butser Hill, popular with hang-gliders and paragliders, with dramatic open downland, yew woods and mixed woodland.

Some 38 butterfly and 12 orchid species have been recorded in the park.

Harting Down

South Harting

Entrance to car park is adjacent to the B2141, approx 1.6km (1 mile) south of South Harting village. (SU790180)
240HA (593ACRES) AONB SSSI
The National Trust

Popular without feeling crowded, Harting Down Local Nature Reserve has been important to man for the last 5,000 years.

A hill fort, dating back to the Iron Age, provides the most obvious signs of the site's history but today the incredible diversity of the site and the exceptional views it provides over the Weald illustrate the importance of the woodland to the local landscape.

Remnants of the downland that was once widespread in this area can be found here, along with mature beech, yew and ash woodland and scrub with numerous flowers that draw birds and butterflies.

There is no circular waymarked trail on the site but it is possible to tackle a DIY circular route using public and permissive paths taking in the varied habitats. There are some very peaceful, sheltered walks in the cross ridge dykes. From here you can gaze over the scrub on the slopes of Round

Down to the mature woodland in the south which is particularly scenic in autumn.

Kingley Vale

West Stoke

Turn west off A286 in Mid Lavant (just north of Chichester) toward West Stoke and through village. On sharp left hand bend take right turn. Car park on right. (SU824088)
150HA (371ACRES) AONB SSSI
English Nature

If you are looking for a different day out, visit Kingley Vale, a fantastic site featuring Britain's finest yew forest.

Though steep in parts, there is a rewarding climb to the top of Box Hill where you can enjoy outstanding panoramic views.

Atmospheric yew woods with some massive old trees dominate the valley slopes. The largest lie at the foot of the valley and their size and dark, contorted shapes add weight to legends of hauntings.

Near the centre of this National Nature Reserve is a yew sculpture representing 'the spirit of Kingley Vale'. You may also discover Bronze Age and Roman earthworks and barrows called the 'Devil's humps' which add archaeological interest.

Signs of roe and fallow deer, stoats, foxes, dormice and

Stansted

badgers can be seen. A host of tree and shrub species support thriving bird populations that include nightingale and green woodpecker while areas of open chalk grassland attract a colourful array of butterflies.

Stansted Forest

Rowlands Castle
From Rowlands Castle, take Woodberry Lane southeast for 2.5km (1.5 miles); then left and left again. Forest car park is 1.6km (1 mile) north on left. (SU753105)
485HA (1,199ACRES)
Stansted Park Foundation

Peaceful and gracious, award-winning Stansted Forest features the longest beech avenue planted on private land in England and boasts some wonderful views of Stansted House.

A site with a host of royal connections, the forest can be traced back to the Roman occupation. In the 11th century a hunting lodge was built for the first Earl of Arundel.

Set around the grounds of Stansted House, the forest won national acclaim in 1995 for its landscape and access improvements, environmentally sound timber production and benefits for wildlife.

Various types of woodland feature alongside open grassland, scrub, wetland and open water. Edged by ancient woodland with huge old trees, are mixed plantations with coppice in the heart of the forest. Access is generally easy over flat rides and paths.

This cocktail of habitats nurtures birds, butterflies and some 250 species of plantlife, including 12 orchid species.

Park Wood

Waterlooville
Just north of Waterlooville toward Horndean, on left opposite The Queens Inclosure. (SU685103)
3HA (7ACRES)
The Woodland Trust

New Forest

New Forest boundary   5 km

Lyndhurst
Between Southampton, Ringwood and
Lymington. Nearest station at
Brockenhurst. (SU300080)
26,500HA (65,497ACRES) AONB SSSI
Forestry Commission

Approached from the sea, the New Forest looks like one vast woodland interrupted by a curious mixture of heavy industry and the villas of the wealthy.

A walk across the forest reveals a much more complex landscape of wild open spaces winding around ancient farmsteads, villages and no fewer than 129 large woods.

The New Forest covers some 375 sq km (145 sq miles). More than 260 sq km is woodland, with one third being enclosed, plantation woodland. The rest is pasture woodland, open heath, bog and grassland.

Today it is criss-crossed by three busy road routes and attracts a staggering seven million visitors a year. Miraculously, the landscape – looking much as it has for 1,500 years – remains a unique place of remarkable peace.

The reason? The New Forest is a forest in the old sense, a place traditionally governed by forest law and not just of trees but incorporating swathes of heathland and forest lawn.

These exceptional pasture woods are maintained by a combination of Forestry Commission management practices and grazing animals owned by commoners exercising their ancient rights in the living tradition of a medieval forest. In season, pigs still roam to feed on acorns and beech mast. Cattle and ponies graze the woodland floor, creating a labyrinth of sunny lawns and glades.

The undoubted stars are the 'ancient and ornamental woods' where the Forestry Commission works to maintain their natural beauty, with minimal intervention.

The size of the forest and the survival of its ancient traditions support an astonishing wealth of wildlife. Even the most determined naturalist could derive a lifetime of pleasure here – and there would still be more to discover.

Located within the busy south of England, the forest is under intense pressure both from developers and for recreational use. Its forthcoming status as a National Park brings hope that a way will be found to secure the forest's special qualities for future generations.

Otterbourne Park Wood

Otterbourne

Junction 12 off M3 toward
Otterbourne. Turn right towards The
Otter pub. 100 metres turn left up lane.
(SU458222)
26HA (64ACRES)
The Woodland Trust

A County Heritage site,
Otterbourne Park Wood
boasts a former Roman road
running through one section,
evidence of which can still be
seen.

Though steep and slippery,
this ancient woodland is well
used by nearby residents and
features oak, ash, maple and
wet valley alders, some of

which are believed to date back
to 1800.

A public footpath runs from
the top of the wood and down
the hill to the northeast corner.

There are large areas of
regeneration where wild
cherry, black poplars, rowan,
sallow and hawthorns are
establishing. Ground cover is
dominated by bracken,
bramble, holly and ivy, dotted
with the typical woodland
sight of yellow pimpernel,
yellow archangel and moschatel.
In wetter areas bugle and
yellow marsh saxifrage thrive
while kingcups and lesser
spearwort abound around the
water.

While in the area, perhaps
extend your visit to nearby
Valley Park Woods in
Chandlers Ford (SU424210).

Otterbourne

Upper Barn & Crowdhill Copses

Bishopstoke

B3354 between Winchester and Botley.
Sharp left turn 1.6km (1 mile) north of
Fair Oak. 100 metres right turn into
Hardings Lane. Keep going to the end
where there is space to park. Walk down
bridleway, right turn into Crowdhill
Copse. (SU484194)
28HA (69ACRES)
The Woodland Trust

Spearywell Woods

Mottisfont, Nr Romsey
Main entrance adjacent to B3084,
approx 6.5km (4 miles) north of
Romsey. (SU315276)
22HA (54ACRES)
The National Trust

Managed by the National Trust
for timber, Spearywell Woods
is a peaceful, easy-to-explore
mixed woodland with all the
ingredients for a great family
day out.

Parts of the wood date back
more than 250 years though
much was planted in the 1930s
and this is reflected in the variety of trees. Stands of tall, elegant young beech trees lead
into mixed woodland of oak,
ash, birch and sweet chestnut
with conifers.

Butterflies such as speckled
wood and the rarer silver-
washed and pearl-bordered
fritillaries frequent the ride
edges in these broadleaved
areas. Then the mood changes
with tall, pure conifer stands
casting deep shadows.

The waymarked route
provides a full six-mile tour of
the estate but you can
complete a circular walk of the
wood in 45 minutes.

Spearywell Woods are part
of the Mottisfont Estate which
includes the ancient woodland
site of Great Copse, a small
and peaceful woodland packed
with wildlife.

Great Copse

Mottisfont, Nr Romsey
On the B3084 approx 6.5km (4 miles)
north of Romsey. Right turning just
north of Spearywell Woods. Or north
from Mottisfont village, turning left
after main entrance to Abbey.
(SU320282)
21HA (52ACRES)
The National Trust

Town and Walters Copse

Porchfield

Take the A3054 Yarmouth to Newport road. Turn left at Shalfleet Garage towards Porchfield. After about 800m (0.5 mile), turn left to Newton. Park in Newtown car park on left, with information point. (SZ430905)
24HA (59ACRES)
The National Trust

You can feel a million miles from civilisation on a visit to Town and Walters Copse.

Quiet and peaceful, the woods are managed as traditional coppice woodlands and sustain a wealth of wildlife including small mammals – especially dormice – and even the red squirrel.

Paths are not waymarked but it's not difficult to find your way if you have your wits about you (but note cyclists are not allowed). The path from the Town Copse entrance leads to an estuary with stunning views where you might spot oyster catcher, shelduck or redshank.

A delightful tunnel of hazel leads on past two contrasting areas, one side wild, dense and seemingly unmanaged. The other a coppiced section, where light can reach the woodland floor, breathing life into bluebells, wood anemones, wood spurge and yellow archangel. In spring, butterflies inhabit more open sections.

In contrast, Walters Copse is more open with wider rides and sections of coppice.

Parkhurst Forest

Newport

Take the A3054 Newport to Yarmouth road. Main entrance is beside two wooden houses, 3km (2 miles) from Newport. (SZ480900)
395HA (976ACRES)
Forestry Commission

Escape to Parkhurst! Forest, that is – for it has the feel of a big wood with cells of contrast, in the sights, sounds and even the smells the visitor can encounter.

A real assortment of conifers and broadleaves, young and old planting and dense and open areas, it has lots to discover.

The conifer stands lining the gravel track are much quieter than the broadleaved areas where you can hear the wind whistling through the leaves. Conifer needles make the ground soft and springy underfoot and their scent is striking, particularly after rain.

Keep your eyes open and you might also spot some carved faces in an old beech coppice tree as you walk along the red squirrel trail and visit the red squirrel viewing hide. Routes are well waymarked, with cycling permitted on the gravel tracks, and you can take advantage of some strategically placed seats.

Firestone Copse

Wootton

Just east of Wootton bridge, turn south-east from the A3054. Follow the Firestone Copse road for 1.6km (1 mile). Car park on right. (SZ559910)

98HA (242ACRES)

Forestry Commission

If you are exploring the area by bike, a slight detour on the 'Round the Island' cycle route takes you through Firestone Copse where cyclists can make use of the gravel tracks.

Those exploring by foot can enjoy the Wootton Creek Trail where heron and water vole may be spotted on the water's edge while buzzards circle overhead.

Mysterious areas of dark pine forest exude wonderfully aromatic smells of pine needles. At the heart of the wood, growing alongside tall pines are majestic redwoods. By contrast the sunny grassy rides are flanked by oak, ash and hazel.

Colourful flowers edge the rides providing food for butterflies such as brimstone and white admiral. Selective thinning of trees has created pockets of light in other areas of the wood.

Situated halfway between Ryde and Cowes on the north of the Island, the area is served by various transport links. The Isle of Wight Steam Railway runs just to the south.

America Wood (see next page)

Borthwood Copse

Apse Heath, Nr Sandown
Take the A3056 from Newport to
Sandown. Turn left at Apse Heath mini
roundabout and the entrance is 800m
(0.5 mile) on right (Alverstone Road).
(SZ567843)
24HA (59ACRES)
The National Trust

A visit to Borthwood Copse
brings many rewards for those
armed with a good sense of
direction. Find your way to
the heart of the wood and you
can enjoy views of the white
chalk of Culver Cliff.

This delightfully natural
ancient woodland does provide
a navigational challenge, not
helped by an ageing information
board which is difficult to
decipher. But persevere – you
will see impressive, large trees
as old as 400 years.

A walk along the sometimes
muddy main path brings an early
reward in the shape of two majestic
beech trees and a big old oak.

In places, Borthwood is
overgrown with bracken and
bramble giving it a wild feel.
Observant visitors might be lucky
to spy red squirrels among the
sweet chestnuts and hazel that
dominate. The taller, more unusual
sessile oak can be found here
growing alongside silver birch,
beech, field maple and holly.

America Wood

Shanklin
Take Apse Manor Road off A3020 just
west of Shanklin. (SZ567820)
11HA (27ACRES) SSSI
The Woodland Trust

It takes a bit of stamina and
determination to get into
America Wood, on the
outskirts of Shanklin, since it
has little accessible parking.

However, the more active Isle
of Wight visitor can make use of
public footpaths and bridleways
that lead into the wood.

There is an 'open' feel to the
site with storm damage in 1987
and 1990 creating lots of open
sections. There is one particularly
large glade which is gradually
reverting to woodland.

While much of the wood is
thought to be ancient, the
northern section has a mixture
of conifers and broadleaves.

Unusually for the Isle of
Wight, most of the wood today
is high oak forest with downy
birch.

The woodland floor supports
a great deal of holly but little
else in the way of ground cover.
Signs of badger and red squirrel
are occasionally spotted.

Mens (see p45)

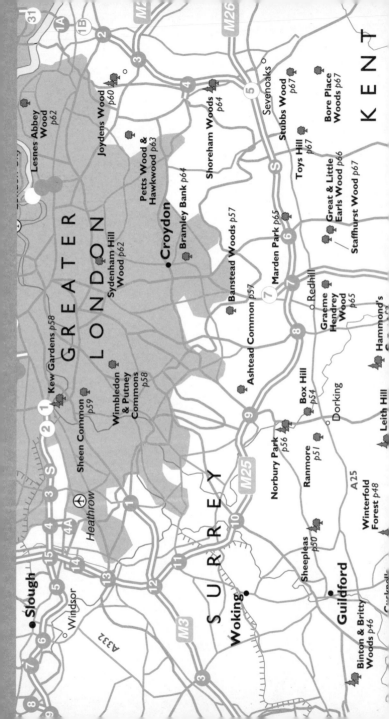

31

1A 1B

M25

M26

2

Lesnes Abbey Wood p62

Joydens Wood p60

4

Sevenoaks 5

Stubbs Wood p67

Bore Place Woods p67

KENT

GREATER

LONDON

Shoreham Woods p64

Petts Wood & Hawkwood p63

Sydenham Hill Wood p62

•Croydon

Bramley Bank p64

Toys Hill p67

Great & Little Earls Wood p66

Staffhurst Wood p67

Kew Gardens p58

Banstead Woods p57

Marden Park p65

6

Sheen Common p59

Wimbledon & Putney Commons p58

Ashtead Common p57

7

Redhill

Graeme Hendrey Wood p65

Heathrow

2 1

2

S

3

Box Hill p54

Dorking

8

9

Hammond's

Norbury Park p56

Leith Hill

15 14 13 12 11

Slough

Windsor

A332

M3

Ranmore p51

A25

Winterfold Forest p48

SURREY

Woking

•

Sheepleas p50

Guildford

•

Binton & Britty Woods p46

M25

10

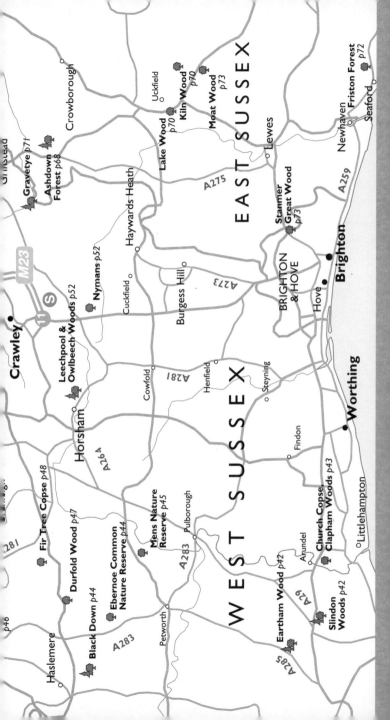

Eartham Wood

Chichester

From Chichester, take the A27 east.
After about 1.6km (1 mile) turn left
onto the A285 to Petworth. Take the
second turning to the right signed
Eartham; the car park is 200m on the
left. (SU936106)
260HA (643ACRES)
Forestry Commission

As public access to Eartham
Wood is not widely promoted,
this commercial beech site is a
quiet place with a number of
attractive features including
pretty vistas.

A gently sloping 1.6 km
(1 mile) waymarked trail follows
paths lined with spring foxgloves
and later with hemp agrimony
and St John's wort through the
woodland.

Pretty in the spring when
light filters through the young
trees, it is good too for autumn
colour. And summer provides
the chance to watch butterflies
feed on the flowering plants in
dappled sunshine.

The waymarked route passes
through a young Norway
spruce plantation before joining
the Monarch's Way footpath,
on the old Stane Street Roman
road, through the beech
plantation where impressive
larch and large, clean stemmed
beech trees line the path.

It is worth combining your
visit with a trip to nearby Selhurst
Park woods which provide
some fantastic views south to
Halnaker Hill and the coast.

Slindon Woods

Slindon

On the A27 north from Chichester, take
the first turning left after the Fontwell
roundabout into Dukes Road. Car park
is 200m on right. Second car park top of
Bignor Hill. (SU952073)
550HA (1359ACRES)
The National Trust

Major changes have taken place
in Slindon Park's extensive
woodland.

In May a sea of bluebells
washes over the woods, making
way for a summer shower of
golden yellow broom and
elegant purple foxgloves.

Once famous for towering
beech trees, many of the greatest
specimens were damaged by
the storms of 1987 and 1990.
A few survived to witness the
wood develop a more diverse
spread of species and see
important new habitats form in
dead and decaying trees.

A remnant deer park, dating
back to the Middle Ages, can
be found at the southern end
and Iron Age field terraces and
a folly can be found in a
section known as the Nore.

More than 20 miles of paths provide access to the site which includes the oak woodland of Slindon Bottom, Longbeat, a beech plantation and Black Jack. The remote and peaceful North Scarp Wood is designated an SSSI.

Church Copse, Clapham Woods

Clapham

Turn off the A280 into Clapham village. At the crossroads turn left to church.

(TQ005067)

10HA (25ACRES) AONB

JF and CC Somerset

Part of larger Clapham Woods, Church Copse's distinctive character has been formed through continued management of hazel by coppicing. Displays of bluebells return each spring

as a reward.

Coppiced wood used to be cut from Church Copse for hurdle making which was used at nearby Findon Sheep Fair during the last century. Dense and mystical groups of large oak trees grow above the hazel, alongside field maple and ash.

A range of footpaths lead visitors up and down the gentle to moderate slopes and, in one place, across a mysterious steep gully. A circular route can be enjoyed but appropriate footwear is required in winter as paths become muddy.

Do not let the absence of a sign or information board at the entrance put you off. This attractive wood is much enjoyed and used by local people. Visitors may witness coppicing in action as BTCV volunteers frequently help the owners with this task.

Blackdown

Black Down

Haslemere
1.6km (1 mile) southeast of Haslemere.
Car parking off Tennyson's Lane on the
northern edge of the property.
(SU920308)
303HA (749ACRES) AONB
The National Trust

At 280 metres – the highest
point in West Sussex – the
wood is a dominant feature of
the local landscape.

With astonishing views,
almost year-round colour and
a wide variety of woodland
birds it is not surprising this
has been regarded as a beauty
spot since Victorian times.

The wettest place in the Weald,
this site offers common,
heathland, ancient and more
recent woodland.

Quellwood Common is a
diverse ancient broadleaved
woodland on Black Down's
southern slopes where two
rock types meet to produce a
hummocky landscape scored
with springs and streams. The
steep, sandy eastern side
supports mature beech woods.

Pine woods cloak much of
the steep slopes of Black Down
where glades add interest. The
best areas of heath – at their
colourful best in summer – are
on the down's southwest flank.

Ebernoe Common Nature Reserve

Northchapel
Take the A283 north from Petworth.
After about 5km (3 miles), take the
minor road right (first road outside the
town). Follow this winding road until
you reach a red phone box. About 10m
further on the right the entrance is
marked 'Ebernoe Church'. (SU976278)
72HA (178ACRES) SSSI
Sussex Wildlife Trust

Historically and ecologically
fascinating, Ebernoe Common
Nature Reserve is an outstanding
example of low Weald woodland.

Remote, teeming with
wildlife, the site has wood pasture with ponds, streams and
flower-rich meadow while
surrounding farmland is being
converted back to woodland.

Lichens – rare outside the
New Forest – thrive here, as do
13 species of British bat,
dormice and a host of birds.

The oak and ash-dominated
site – hit by the storms of 1987
– now features a wide age range
of trees including some beautiful, gnarled ancient specimens.
The rides and glades support
many floral species.

Remnants of a small brickworks
can be seen on the common
including the brick kiln, now a
scheduled ancient monument.

Visitors are advised to go

Ebernoe

The Mens Nature Reserve is something of an ancient wilderness where Nature has been allowed to reign unchallenged for more than a century.

Once used for timber production, woodland management of the site was abandoned about 120 years ago, leaving it to grow untamed.

There is much to discover here – there is a waymarked trail from the car park but wear sturdy boots since the paths are often narrow and muddy – even in summer.

Huge, towering beech stand out in a woodland with trees of all sizes and ages. Notable among the oaks is the vast Idehurst Oak with a girth of more than six metres.

Open areas are few but Badlands Meadow in the southeast has an impressive display of summer flowers including lady's mantle and dyers greenwood.

The site sustains a wealth of birds and butterflies – including nuthatch, blackcap, woodpecker as well as purple emperor, white admiral and silver washed fritillary butterflies.

prepared with sturdy boots and a plan – while flat, it is often wet underfoot and the plethora of paths can make it difficult to find your way.

Mens Nature Reserve

Petworth

Take the A272 east from Petworth. After about 6.5km (4 miles), turn right at crossroads in the middle of a large wood, signposted Hawkhurst Court. Car park is about 100m on right. (TQ023237) 159HA (393ACRES) AONB SSSI
Sussex Wildlife Trust

Binton &
Britty Woods

Farnham

South of the A31 and west of the A3.
Head south from Seale towards Elstead.
Car parking is on the right just before
crossroads with Littleworth Road, after
about 800m (0.5 mile). (SU895465)
100HA (247ACRES) AONB

Hampton Estate

Spring is a good time to visit
the Hampton Estate when
bluebells add a splash of colour
to the woodland landscape of
Binton and Britty woods.

A circular walk connects
both of the woods, which are
commercially managed for
timber production, with
wooded Puttenham Common
and the North Downs Way.

The bluebells grow in
Binton, a 41-hectare site with a
clear 'north-south' division –
the northern side dominated
by sweet chestnut coppice
while the south is given over to
pine, fir and larch.

A waymarked trail on the
easy, sandy soils of Binton
can be completed in about an
hour, providing plenty of
opportunity to move on to
neighbouring Britty Wood.

Occasional oaks and Corsican
pines dot the landscape of this
62-hectare site which is

dominated by Scots pine. A
single main route weaves
through its central shallow
valley with occasional woodland
paths providing additional
opportunities to explore its
gentle to moderate slopes.

Witley Common

Witley

11km (7 miles) southwest of Guildford
between the A3 and the A286. 1.6km
(1 mile) southwest of Milford.
Signposted from A3. (SU933407)
152HA (376ACRES) AONB SSSI

The National Trust

Visitors – particularly children
– can get fun out of their
hands on experience of nature
while the grown ups enjoy a
leisurely stroll around Witley
Common.

This National Trust site, a
combination of heathland,
woodland, scrub, grassland and
ponds, has good recreation,
education and interactive
facilities, including a children's
nature trail.

Easy walking along some
well maintained waymarked
trails provides access to the
heathland of Witley Common
(where three types of heather
create eye-catching late
summer colour) and to mixed
woodland which has evolved

over 60 years on land formerly used for grazing.

Impressive tall stands of Scots pine and imposing large sweet chestnuts alternate with grassy areas and glades, one of which was used as a parade ground by troops during both world wars.

The woods support three species of woodpecker. The wheelchair accessible visitor centre, which hosts excellent children's events, provides further information.

Durfold Wood

Dunsfold

From Chiddingfold village green head southeast on Pickhurst Road which becomes Fisher Lane. About half a mile before a right hand bend and 100m before the Plaistow Road T-junction, turn sharp right into small car park. (SU987326)

18HA (44ACRES) AONB SSSI

The Woodland Trust

War games were once played among the oak trees of Durfold Wood but today it is a peaceful part of the Surrey countryside.

Set well away from main roads, it is a light and airy site within the much larger Chiddingfold Forest Site of Special Scientific Interest.

Durfold

Man has made numerous changes to this ancient woodland over the years, practically clearing it during both world wars. Therefore few very old trees remain.

Dormice, butterflies and moths, reptiles, insects and birds thrive here, among them woodcock, tawny owl, lesser spotted woodpecker and even nightingales.

Work to improve habitats includes tree thinning, ride widening and traditional hedge laying. The public bridleway across the southern end connects with the Sussex Border Path.

Oldbury

Winterfold Forest

Albury

From the A254 Guildford to Dorking
road, take the A248 (signposted
Godalming). After 800m (0.5 mile) cross
small bridge, then turn left into New
Road up hill over level crossing to
Farley Green, then left at village green
into Shophouse Lane, then 1.6km (1 mile)
to forest sign. (TQ065435)
135HA (334ACRES) AONB
Mr J A McAllister

No matter how many times
you return to Winterfold
Forest, part of the extensive
Hurt Wood area of the North
Downs, there is always more
to explore.

Mainly privately owned, it
has been open to the public for
almost 80 years. Thirty miles
of public rights of way run
through the site plus another
30 miles of unofficial tracks
and a choice of 12 car parks

Hurt Wood – named after
the bilberry or 'hurts' that
grow here – covers more than
1,200 hectares of heath and
woodland on the greensand
ridge. From the southern
escarpment ridge, among fine
tall beech trees, are panoramic
views across the Weald.

The slope is broken by valleys
and streams where oak, birch,
rowan and sweet chestnut,
abound. Elsewhere, tall Scots
pine dominate with bracken
and bilberry providing autumn
colour at their feet.

Fir Tree Copse

Godalming/Haslemere

Southeast of Dunsfold on road to
Alford Crossways and Horsham, take
second right turn after 3km (2 miles)

into Rams Lane. Follow car park signs to Forestry Commission site at Sidney Wood. (TQ023350)
6HA (14ACRES) SSSI
Surrey Wildlife Trust

Perfect for a peaceful interlude, Fir Tree Copse is a quiet woodland in the heart of a much larger wooded habitat.

Beautiful, tall straight oak and ash trees dominate the site with hazel coppice beneath. Light and shade is created thanks to a programme of recoppicing which has formed glades, allowing light back onto the woodland floor.

A distinctive, small clump of Scots pine which stands in its southwestern section probably gives the wood its name.

Colour comes from a host of woodland flowers including bluebell, wood anemone, dog's mercury, enchanter's nightshade, pignut, lily of the valley and wild daffodil. Further interest is provided by marshland species that grow on the northwest boundary, site of the now derelict Wey and Arun Canal.

Routes through the site are well waymarked on passable, if narrow paths. A round tour takes just 30 minutes, leaving ample time to explore surrounding woodland.

Cucknells Wood □

Godalming
Turn off B2128 about 1.6km (1 mile) southeast of Shamley Green into Stroud Lane. The wood is on the left after 500m. (TQ041430)
10HA (25ACRES)
Surrey Wildlife Trust

Bluebell, foxglove, primrose, common spotted orchid – just some of the many flowers on show in this peaceful wood.

Narrow paths wind around large oaks, ash, birch and rowan, coppiced hazel, holly, wild cherry and crab apple. In the centre is a group of Norway spruce planted as Christmas trees.

Northwards the landscape becomes wetter with a carpet of soft mosses growing beneath alders. Snake's Alley, a damp open space in the northwest, supports a good range of insect life.

In spring migrant birds, including chiff-chaff, willow warbler and blackcap, join the resident population of nuthatch, marsh and willow tits, tawny owl, tree creeper and three woodpecker species.

A waymarked walk offers a pleasant half hour stroll. Nearby Winterfold Wood provides a wonderful contrast in scale and character.

Sheepleas

Between West and East Horsley
From Leatherhead take the A246 to
East Horsley. In East Horsley turn
south into Chalk Lane and then right
into Greendene where the car park can
be found on the right. Alternatively,
continue on the A246 through East
Horsley and park in the car park in
Epsom Road adjacent to St Mary's
Church. (TQ080514)
108HA (267ACRES) AONB SSSI
Surrey Wildlife Trust

One could easily get lost in the
maze of permissive paths and
rights of way that weave through
this section of the North Downs.

There is a great variety of
habitats including mature beech
and oak woodland, plantations,
hazel coppice, scrub and
meadow with two waymarked
trails (if occasionally
confusing) and a self-guided
circular trail.

Close to the car park is a picnic
area and, not far from here, a
Millennium viewpoint offering
views extending to Canary
Wharf, the Telecom Tower and
other London landmarks.

Renowned for its chalkland
flora, the site supports quaking
grass, rock rose, eyebright,
milkwort, common spotted
and fragrant orchids. In the
mixed woodland you'll find
coppiced sections, yew and
box walks, some magnificent
beeches and attractive glades
animated with butterflies by
day and bats at night.

Common blue, green
hairstreak, grizzled skipper
and silver washed fritillary are
among the 30 species of
butterfly recorded here.

Leith Hill

Ranmore

Dorking

3km (2 miles) northwest of Dorking on road to East Horsley. Adjacent to southern boundary of Polesden Lacey Estate on A246 2.5km (1.5 miles) from Bookham. (TQ142504)
266HA (657ACRES) AONB SSSI
The National Trust

This ancient wooded common on the North Downs is a local landmark.

Huge mature beech, oak and yew trees adorn the slopes of the downs, divided by gently sloping wooded valleys.

There is something to enjoy all year round in this cool, quiet and peaceful site where a variety of paths provide a network through wide and open areas and beneath the closed canopy of trees. The going can get wet and muddy – so sturdy footwear is recommended.

Even though access doesn't appear to be actively promoted, this is a woodland to be enjoyed by all. Visitors without transport of their own can use the local explorer bus or walk from Polesden Lacey through Ranmore.

Nearby is the Woodland Trust's 28 HA (70 acres) Great Ridings Wood (TQ105539).

Leith Hill

Coldharbour, Dorking

Northwest of the A29; west of the A24; south of the A25. (TQ132428)
270HA (667ACRES) AONB SSSI
The National Trust

Close to the conifer plantations of Abinger and Wotton Commons is tower-topped Leith Hill from where, on a clear day, you can see across 13 counties.

The hill is served by lots of paths and tracks – many of them steep and rough. Athletic visitors can tackle the strenuous climb through the woods to the base of the Leith Hill tower.

During spring and summer the southern slopes are ablaze with rhododendron planted in 1900 by Charles Darwin's sister, Caroline Wedgwood.

Beech and pine grows in steep gulleys on the scarp face but the main woodland – birch, oak and beech – lies on the greensand ridge. Particularly stunning is Severells Copse with beautiful oak over birch coppice.

The arboretum either side of the Coldharbour has some impressive redwoods and exotic species to marvel at.

Nightjars, adders and lizards are making their homes in newly created glades.

Leechpool & Owlbeech Woods

Horsham

To the east of Horsham town centre just off the B2195 (Harwood Road).
(TQ194314)
34HA (84ACRES)
Horsham District Council

Roe deer can be spotted in both these contrasting woods which are served by two way-marked routes.

Leechpool is a mixed wood-land of oak, beech, sweet chestnut, Scots pine and holly where a good variety of spring flowering plants and a whole range of birds add interest.

Contrasting Owlbeech is made up of conifers and heath-land, with cool alders, ferns and mosses. It supports a variety of birds and visiting fallow deer. A stream running through the wood sustains amphibians and dragonflies.

The site is well served by formal and informal paths – occasionally muddy – and well-maintained boardwalks over the wet areas.

The High Weald Landscape Trail crosses St Leonard's Forest (almost adjoining), a large Forestry Commission plantation including Scots and Corsican pine.

Nymans

Handscross

On the B2114 at Handcross, just off the London to Brighton (M23/A23) road.
(TQ265297)
100HA (247 ACRES) AONB SSSI
The National Trust

There are a number of enjoyable walks through this exceptional woodland.

The woods, which occupy 100 hectares of the 243 hectare estate, lie in the valley and are accessible only via steep slopes and steps.

Used at various times to serve the iron, leather tanning and boat-building industries, the woods today are peaceful and well maintained – managed for public access and wildlife, which thrives among the gnarled old beeches and oaks of the steep-sided ghylls.

Close to a delightful avenue of tall conifers can be found Sussex's third tallest tree – a wellingtonia – which lost its tallest title after lightning destroyed its top in the 1990s.

Three waymarked routes through ancient woodland, conifer plantations and beside a large central lake are extended in spring to include a bluebell walk through Pookchurch wood.

Hammond's Copse

Newdigate

From A24/A25 roundabout in Dorking take A24 south and left into Chart Lane. After 1.6km (1 mile) turn left into Red Lane. At next T-junction turn right and right again at next T-junction and right into Broad Lane. Copse on your left, two entrances, better parking at southern entrance next to derelict chapel. (TQ212441)

30HA (74ACRES)

The Woodland Trust

An opportunity to find out how good management can return ancient woodland sites such as this to their former glory.

There are more than 5.5km (3.5 miles) of well-maintained paths ranging from open sunny rides to mysterious narrow routes deep in the heart of the wood and a waymarked nature trail.

A large pond with a marshy area at the centre of the wood is home to dragonflies and newts. On your walk listen for tawny owls, watch sparrowhawks in flight and catch a glimpse of colourful butterflies such as silver-washed fritillary, yellow brimstone and white admiral.

In spring migrant chiffchaffs and blackcaps sing above colourful splashes of bluebell and wild daffodil. Look also for guelder rose, wild service tree and wood spurge – all species typical of ancient woodland. An information leaflet is available to guide visitors.

There are three other Woodland Trust sites nearby you may also like to visit: Glover's Wood (TQ227406), Edolph's Copse (TQ236424) and Rickett's Wood (TQ230428).

Nymans

Box Hill

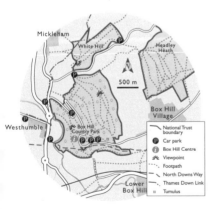

Dorking

From the A24, turn east on to B2209 at
Westhumble. Turn east after 400m (0.25
mile) – signed to Box Hill. (TQ180513)
217HA (536ACRES) AONB SSSI
The National Trust

More than a million visitors a year flock to Box Hill, a beautiful blend of downland and woodland that dominates the countryside north of Dorking.

Dotted with many interesting features, this is an historic site. As well as two Bronze Age burial mounds, the Roman road of Stane Street linking Chichester with London crosses the site. Remains of a Romano-British settlement have been discovered nearby.

Box Hill fort, constructed in 1899, was built to help protect London from the threat of invasion. Today it is colonised by several species of bat. John Logie Baird conducted his TV experiments at the summit.

Dramatic scarp slopes, known as the Whites, rise up from the River Mole where stepping stones indicate an ancient crossing point.

Teeming with birds, bats and butterflies as well as people, it features no fewer than 400 species of flowering plant and 58 species of butterfly. Generations of visitors have enjoyed the stunning views from its busy summit – one of the highest points on the North Downs.

Woodland covers more than half the site. Named after the renowned box trees that grow on its steep chalk slopes, the plateau area also supports oak and ash with wild cherry, birch and rowan. There are beautiful large beech and magnificent yews, some estimated to be over 250 years old.

Designated a Country Park in 1971, facilities today are good with an information centre, shop, picnic area, café and a choice of car parks. Children will enjoy the family fun trail and summer events.

At particularly busy times it is probably best to avoid the summit and explore further afield. There are many alternatives to choose from including a number of waymarked routes ranging from 1–5 hours. Leaflets describing each route, including a two-hour nature trail, are available from the shop.

The attractive mix of grazed downland, woodland and views has attracted visitors here over the centuries making it one of the southeast's honeypot destinations. Many of the fine, old beech and yew trees were but saplings when the first modern-day 'tourists' arrived in the 17th century but the storms of 1987 and 1990 took their toll. Where these fell, natural regeneration has been allowed to take over and scrub species such as whitebeam, hawthorn and dog rose are now taking their place.

Norbury Park

Leatherhead

From the A24 south of Leatherhead turn west at the roundabout onto the A246 towards Fetcham. Young Street car park is on the left just before the railway bridge. Or continue on A246 and take first left on roundabout at top of hill for Fetcham and Bocketts Farm car parks. (TQ158538)

526HA (1,300ACRES) AONB SSSI

Surrey County Council

Recreation, relaxation and education are all well catered for at Norbury Park.

This popular site combines multi-purpose woodland, farmland and chalk grassland offering wonderful views and excellent access. The various features to be found here include a three-hour woodland management demonstration trail illustrating how the site is being managed for timber production, wildlife conservation and visitors alike.

The woodland and chalk grassland area is a designated SSSI featuring yew, ash, cherry, oak, hazel and sweet chestnut coppice and an ancient yew section known as Druids Grove. Some areas were hit by the storms of '87 which opened the way for new planting.

Public and permissive routes, a self-guided circular trail, permanent orienteering course and family off-road cycle route all help to keep the most active visitor busy. Thought to be one of the Mickleham manors mentioned in the Domesday Book, Norbury was purchased by Surrey County Council to shield it from development.

Ashstead Common

Ashtead Common

Ashtead

Approaching Ashtead from A24, turn down Woodfield Lane opposite Leg of Mutton and Cauliflower pub. Continue down lane for 800m, over two mini roundabouts towards rail station. Over level crossing, turn left, park on side of road, Common lies ahead. (TQ180590) 210HA (500ACRES) SSSI

Corporation of London

Ashtead Common is a fabulous mosaic of grassland, wetland, scrub and woodland boasting magnificent old trees.

Set on a ridge, with views across the surrounding landscape, good paths lead visitors through a succession of habitats.

For centuries, around 2,000 ancient oaks – some up to 400 years old – have been cropped to manage the wood. Many of these mature fungi-clad pollards are riddled with nooks and crannies providing homes for bats, owls, woodpeckers, tree creepers and nuthatches. This deadwood sustains 1,000 species of beetle, 150 of them rare.

While in the area, Ashtead Park is also worth a visit with its veteran trees, woodland, meadows and ponds.

Banstead Woods

Chipstead/Banstead

Follow the B2219 (Holly Lane) from Banstead for 3km (2 miles). Large car park on right. (TQ273593) 115HA (284ACRES) SSSI

Reigate and Banstead Borough Council

Popular with walkers, joggers, children and dog owners, beautiful Banstead is a joy to discover – though the hour or so it takes to cover the site throws up some challenging inclines.

There is a grand feeling to this large ancient woodland set on the edge of a steep slope. It boasts commanding views of the local landscape.

The site features some big old oaks and beech trees along with sweet chestnuts, silver birch, wild cherries and coppiced hazel. At the top of the wood there is a small woodland pond.

Despite the numbered way-marker posts, you can get lost in Banstead but thanks to the grid-like system of paths you're soon back on track. Most of the paths are wide and compacted, lending a sense of space and grandness.

Cycling and horse riding is not permitted in the wood.

Wimbledon & Putney Commons

Wimbledon
Take Windmill Road, off Parkside
(A219). Road leads to golf clubhouse
and the windmill. (TQ221720)
456HA (1,127ACRES) SSSI
**The Board of Wimbledon & Putney
Commons Conservators (W&PCC)**

Wimbledon and neighbouring
Putney commons have all you
could ask for an enjoyable day
'wandering free'.

Here you will discover areas
of oak and birch, beech and
hornbeam woodland,
heathland with large lakes and
ponds, man-made ponds and
acidic spring bogs – a range of
landscapes for visitors on foot,
horseback and cycle to explore.

The extensive mature woodland and open space makes it
easy to forget you are just a
stone's throw from Central
London and feel as though you
are in the countryside. Low-
flying golf balls can let you
know that courses are nearby.

While there is a good
network of well-surfaced paths,
it is possible to lose your way.
The woodland is a wonderful
area with big and beautiful oak
and beech contrasting with
areas of dense undergrowth.
This is a great place to enjoy
bluebells in spring.

*Wimbledon Common,
Robin Hood Ride*

The open grassland is good
for ground nesting birds
during late spring and early
summer.

Kew Gardens

Richmond
Enter by Brentford Gate via Kew Green
and Ferry Lane. Other entrances – Main
Gate (off Kew Green), Victoria Gate
(off Kew Road) and Lion Gate (off Kew
Road). (TQ189768)
49HA (121ACRES)
Royal Botanic Gardens Kew

Very different and much more formal than other sites featured in this guide, Kew will be of considerable interest to anyone who enjoys woodland and trees.

As well as visiting the glasshouses and flower gardens, a couple of hours spent in the more wooded western part of the grounds will be a rewarding experience. This area has a parkland feel with many native and exotic trees growing over mown grass.

A riverside walk with good views over the Thames leads through birch, chestnuts and poplars and past some fine oaks. In the northwestern corner is a conservation area managed as native woodland and famed for its carpet of bluebells each May.

A stroll around the grounds brings constant surprises – around the next corner could be an imposing giant redwood or an unusually elegant conifer. A 'deadwood felled area' has been created as a landscape feature and a habitat for wildlife, particularly stag beetles.

Sheen Common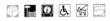

Richmond

From A205 Richmond Road, take B351 Sheen Lane. Turn right onto Christchurch Road and at mini round-about go straight on to Fife Road. Park on roadside as road bends to left. Keep playing fields on left and enter wood. (TQ197745)

21HA (52ACRES)

London Borough of Richmond

Just a stone's throw from the delights of Richmond Park lies the dense woodland of Sheen Common, a haven for wildlife.

Though rich in trees, there are still patches of grassland with wild heather in open glades, lending an open feel. The area is a favourite haunt of dog owners and a popular gateway into the park, with a good network of paths.

The area was an open common used for grazing until the 1930s but, since then, has become rich in rowan, holly and sycamore, has some beautifully shaped oaks with open crowns and a 150-year-old plane tree.

Observant visitors might spot foxes, woodpeckers, speckled wood butterflies and even badgers. The pond in the northern section of the site is good for frogs, toads and beetles, despite the sometimes orange hue of the water caused by iron deposits in the soil.

Joydens Wood

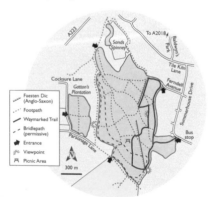

Map Legend

- ▦▦ Faesten Dic (Anglo-Saxon)
- --- Footpath
- —— Waymarked Trail
- ⊸⊸ Bridlepath (permissive)
- 🏠 Entrance
- ☀ Viewpoint
- ⛺ Picnic Area

300 m

Bexley South (Greater London)
Southeast London, west of A2018 south
of Old Bexley. (TQ501717)
135HA (333ACRES)
The Woodland Trust

Set on a hilltop just 21km (13 miles) from the heart of London, is Joydens Wood.

Look carefully and you will see relics of its history including banks, ditches, humps and hollows beneath the trees and the remains of two late Iron Age roundhouses which are more than 2,000 years old. The Faesten Dic, meaning 'the strong dike', is believed to be an Anglo-Saxon defensive bank and ditch. A gravel path on the eastern edge suggests this was once patrolled. You can follow this north to south through the wood along a clearly marked 3 km trail with boardwalks in wetter areas.

In the centre of the woods a series of banks or lynchets provides evidence that the area was farmed in the Middle Ages. Small depressions in the ground indicate deneholes where underlying chalk was mined and spread on fields to try and improve the poor soil. Not being very productive land it was abandoned by farming and trees reclaimed the soil.

A leaflet produced jointly by the Woodland Trust and the Archaeological Unit of Cambridgeshire County Council explains how, for thousands of years, people have been altering Joydens Wood to suit their different purposes.

This hilly site is popular with local walkers and is open for cycling on 5.5km of tracks and a permit riding scheme extending along 4km.

Despite being replanted with Corsican pine in the 1950s, the site has a wide variety of native trees, shrubs and flowers which the owners are working to increase. Coppicing and clearing of the rides is helping to create a more open character to the wood.

As more light enters the wood, increased flowers, butterflies, birds and insects appear. Wood ants are one of many minibeasts that respond well to the increased sunlight, to the delight of green woodpeckers, which catch them on their long sticky tongues. A colourful collection of fungi can also be found.

All three British newts species are to be found in the numerous ponds which dot the site, including the rare Great Crested Newt.

Chalk Wood, to the south, is ancient woodland dominated by oak, silver birch and sweet chestnut and well worth a visit.

Lesnes Abbey Wood

Belvedere
Abbey Road (B213) is to east of A2041
in Belvedere. (TQ478787)
88HA (217ACRES) SSSI
Bexley Council

Lesnes Abbey is a treasure
trove of natural and
archaeological discoveries
where you can forget the
bustle of the nearby capital.

The broadleaved woodland
around the abbey ruins
includes impressive hornbeam
and unusual exotics. It comes
alive in warmer months with
bluebells and wild daffodils in
spring and colourful St John's
wort, willow herbs and yellow
archangel in the summer.

Woodpeckers, kestrels and
tawny owls share the woods,
unusually, with ring necked
parakeets. Yellow iris, reedmace,
frogs and the occasional grey
heron can be spotted around
the ponds.

Self-guided trails around the
site offer good views across the
Thames towards London and
include interesting features
such as 'Sleeping Dryad' – a
sweet chestnut with a face.

Venture into open heathland
in the heart of the wood and
look for butterflies, insects and
birds. The mounds here are
thought to be the remains of an
ancient burial site. In some
sections fossils have been
uncovered.

Sydenham Hill Wood

Upper Sydenham
The main entrance is in Crescent Wood
Road, SE26, off Sydenham Hill.
(TQ344724)
10HA (25ACRES)
London Wildlife Trust

Those with an interest in
wildlife or history will reap
rewards on a visit to Sydenham
Hill Wood – a site with plenty
of variety and interest.

Part of the Great North
Wood, an ancient woodland
straddling the ridge between
Deptford, Streatham and
Selhurst, it is a great place for
butterflies in the summer.

Quite dense in places, there
are contrasting, more open
clearings where trees – oaks,
hornbeam, sycamore and ash
among them – have fallen in
storms.

Numbered posts – not the
easiest to follow – take visitors
on a figure of eight tour of the
wood, part of which was once
incorporated into the gardens
of Victorian villas. Little
remains of these old houses

today but you might discover the remains of an old tennis court and Victorian folly.

Dead wood, left for the benefit of wildlife, provides nesting places for the lesser spotted woodpeckers – look out too for bullfinches and hawfinches.

Petts Wood & Hawkwood

Chislehurst

Park in Chislehurst and walk southeast along the main road A208. The woods lie to the southwest of the road.
(TQ450687)
134HA (331ACRES)
The National Trust

Petts Wood

Surprisingly peaceful woodland where the sound of birdsong helps you escape the noise of nearby traffic.

There is a variety of tree species including some big old pollarded oaks and young emerging trees.

Within the woods clearings have been maintained as part of a heathland creation project where dead standing trees provide wonderful nesting posts and insect habitats.

The west of the wood overlooks Tongs Farm, an open meadow where sheep graze, and produces a wonderful show of wildflowers.

The wood is surrounded by Chiselhurst and St Paul's Cray commons with Scadbury Nature Reserve just over the road.

Bramley Bank

Croydon
Main entrance at bottom of Riesco
Drive, off Ballards Way, South
Croydon. Limited car parking in Riesco
Drive or in large District Council car
park on left of Riesco Drive.
(TQ352634)
11HA (27ACRES)
London Wildlife Trust

This is a well-walked wood
with a circular route allowing
visitors to enjoy a host of
interesting features including
great views over nearby fields
to more distant, urban
landscapes.

The London Loop follows
the eastern side of the wood
and is waymarked. Clear and
well-trodden paths lead by
large oaks and at least one
majestic looking beech to a
large pond in the northern
section. A little murky and
shaded, it is lined with lilies
and supports a number of
moorhens and other wildlife.

Elsewhere, look for standing
deadwood trunks which display
markings of woodpeckers and
burrowing insects.

The mature woodland is
populated with sycamore, sweet
chestnut, ash, and silver birch
standing above bramble, bracken
and young regenerating trees.

Shoreham Woods

Shoreham
11km (7 miles) north of Sevenoaks off
A224. J4 off M25, take A224 to Dunton
Green. At next roundabout take first
exit, Shacklands Road to Shoreham. Car
park 250m on right. (TQ501616)
101HA (250ACRES) AONB
Sevenoaks District Council

A network of footpaths enable
you to explore the woods of
Jenkins Neck, Barnetts,
Meenfield, Pilots and Andrew's
Wood, an ancient woodland site.

Conifer plantations are being
thinned and replanted with
broadleaves. Look out for a
magnificent beech tree
surrounded by younger trees and
a beautifully carved seat on the
eastern side of Andrew's Wood.

Across the motorway, areas
of oak have dense vegetation
beneath contrasting with the
neighbouring beech.

To the east of Meenfield
Wood, wonderful views extend
over the Darent Valley toward
Shoreham village. Look for a
memorial cross cut into the
hillside.

The varied bird population
includes tree creeper, chaffinch
and kestrel. Look out for
purple hairstreak and white
admiral butterflies.

Marden Park

Woldingham
Follow Northdown Road, south of
Woldingham and right into Gangers
Hill. Car park on right after S-bend. If
coming from M25, take junction 6 and
A22 south. At roundabout turn left
onto A25. After 800m turn left into
Tandridge Hill Lane. At T-junction
right into Gangers Hill, car park on left.
(TQ369539)
63HA (156ACRES) AONB SSSI
The Woodland Trust

Marden

High on the South Downs,
within the Surrey Hills Area of
Outstanding Natural Beauty,
you will find Marden Park Woods,
the largest site owned by the
Woodland Trust in the county.

This expanse of varying
woodland habitats – quite a
draw for visitors – is actually
made up of Marden Park and
Great Church Wood.

This is an area of great diversity
from ancient woodland to
large expanses of developing
woods and stretches of
recreated chalk grassland
where plants such as common,
bee and greater butterfly
orchids thrive.

As a result this is a rich
haven of wildlife with no fewer
than 25 species of butterfly,
rare snails and stripe-winged
grasshoppers.

The North Downs Way and
the six-mile Woldingham
Countryside Walk both run
through the site which is well
served by an extensive network
of maintained permissive
footpaths while a surfaced
bridleway allows riders a safe
route through part of the
woods.

Graeme Hendrey Wood

Bletchingley
Take Rabies Heath Road east from
Bletchingley. Park in Tilburstow Hill
car park on right. (TQ346501)
10HA (25ACRES)
Surrey Wildlife Trust

Great & Little Earls Wood

Oxted

In Limpsfield take Wolf's Row south, off A25. Road becomes Pollards Wood and then Reed Lane. Just after Merle Common Road joins from right, woodland appears on right. Near Royal Oak pub on left is parking and entrance with an information board.

(TQ406489)

10HA (25ACRES) SSSI

The Woodland Trust

The ancient woodlands of Great & Little Earls Woods form the western extremity of a much larger expanse of woodland in this area. Most is designated a Site of Special Scientific Interest.

Sweet chestnut is still coppiced in the south of Great Earls Wood but this gives way to a high forest of oak and sweet chestnut in the north. Little Earls Wood to the north-west has a delightful area of old hornbeam coppice.

Great & Little Earls are locally known for their fantastic display of bluebells in spring. Bracken, honeysuckle and creeping soft grass are also abundant and grow alongside a number of ancient woodland indicator species.

A small pond is located in the centre of a recently created conservation ride and this is fed by a seasonal stream which runs the length of the ride.

Visitors benefit from a good network of well-maintained paths and three information boards.

Toys Hill

Toys Hill

Westerham

4km (2.5 miles) south of Brasted, 1.6km (1 mile) west of Ide Hill. Car park close to the Fox & Hounds public house. (TQ465517)

194HA (479ACRES) SSSI

The National Trust

The storms that lashed Britain in 1987 changed the face of Toys Hill and their legacy is evident today.

Designated of national importance for nature conservation, it is part of a band of hilltop woods and sustains a good selection of woodland plants, birds and mammals. Rich in insects and fauna, it also produces an excellent selection of fungi in the autumn.

Much of the site's storm-damaged timber was cleared but around a quarter was left to rot, to encourage wildlife. The worst-hit sections – on the plateau – are now regenerating vigorously while lower down, mature oak, birch and pine grow in a sheltered and tranquil vale.

In contrast, the north and east facing slopes of the site – at 235 metres Kent's highest point – suffered little damage and here you can enjoy the full beauty of Toys Hill as it was pre-1987. Longer routes through the site lead to beautiful mature woodland.

Stubbs Wood (Hanging Bank)

Ide Hill

800m (0.5 mile) east of Ide Hill along the B2042, turn right on minor road at T-junction. Parking 450m on right. (TQ498518)

40HA (99ACRES)

Kent County Council

Staffhurst Wood

Oxted

From A25 south through Limpsfield Common to Grants Lane (TQ4714485)

38HA (94ACRES) SSSI

**Surrey Wildlife Trust/
The Woodland Trust**

Bore Place Woods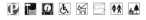

Chiddingstone

Take the B2027 which runs between Edenbridge and Tonbridge and follow the signposts to Bore Place. (TQ505490)

20HA (49ACRES)

Commonwork

Ashdown Forest

**Uckfield, Crowborough,
East Grinstead**
A22 to Wych Cross crossroads, turn
east for 1.6km (1 mile) to Forest Centre.
(TQ433324)
2467HA (6,097ACRES) AONB SSSI
Ashdown Forest Trust

Centuries of change, natural and man-made, have helped to shape the 10 square miles of heathland and woodland that make up Ashdown Forest, a site drawing more than a million visitors annually.

Visitors are well catered for with 50 car parks, extensive rides and footpaths, activities such as horse riding (with a permit), kite flying – even golf – and a Forest Centre. Yet a short walk is all it takes to transport the visitor to quieter areas of beauty.

Wildlife thrives at Ashdown, with a sizeable bird population including nightjar and woodcock, no fewer than 34 different butterfly species and around half Britain's 46 breeding species of damselflies and dragonflies.

Heathland – the largest expanse in the southeast and nearly 5 per cent of all that remains in Britain – is the star attraction here. Stunningly beautiful, it supports some of the country's rarest wildlife and an abundance of colourful heathers.

A forest in the oldest sense of the word, Ashdown was created for deer hunting and today supports four different species.

Woodland, which makes up around 40 per cent of the site, is extensive. While most woods on the site were cleared at some time to make charcoal for the iron industry, a handful are believed to be ancient. Today there is a wide variety of trees: pendunculate oak and silver birch are interspersed with beech, birch and sycamore, sweet chestnut, field maple, ash and hazel and clumps of Scots pine, planted in the 19th century.

Older sections are richest in flora while damper sections of the woods have an abundance of ferns including the rare marsh fern, found on just a few other sites in Sussex.

A A Milne used the Forest's wonderful settings as inspiration for the many adventures of Winnie the Pooh.

Lake Wood

Lake Wood

Uckfield
Follow Church Street, west out of
Uckfield. Parking in lay-by opposite
wood in Rocks Road. (TQ463217)
8HA (20ACRES)
The Woodland Trust

A magical combination of
water and trees gave Lake
Wood its name and inspired
generations of visitors.

In the 18th century the
Streatfield family landscaped the
site in the style of Capability
Brown, creating a large lake
and nearby water garden
planted with exotic trees and
shrubs.

Rocky sandstone outcrops,
with high cliffs overhanging
the water, add to the dramatic
beauty. A tunnel cut through
the rock completes the path
around the lake which supports
an interesting fish population
and the impressive royal fern,
rare elsewhere in Sussex.

The storm of 1987 created
chaos but since the Woodland
Trust took over a decade ago,
much has been done to arrest
an invasion of rhododendron.

Much of the wood is still
ancient coppice supporting a
wide variety of ancient woodland flowers and a fascinating
wildlife population. Lake
Wood is home to dormice and
almost 60 species of bird –
including kingfisher and heron.

Kiln Wood

Blackboys
B2192 south of Blackboys, turn into
Hollow Lane, entrance 400m on left.
(TQ522201)
9HA (22ACRES) AONB
The Woodland Trust

Kiln Wood illustrates the need to protect our precious remnants of ancient woodland.

Look for bluebells, lords and ladies, wood anemone and garlic mustard – species which indicate an area of ancient woodland. These can be found in one third of the site. Adjoining this are two areas of new native woodland planted to help protect and extend this rare and important habitat.

While mostly easy going, the land then gently slopes towards a stream which runs from the northeast diagonally through the wood to exit adjacent to the woodland entrance.

The high forest canopy overhead is dominated by mature oak with lesser amounts of sycamore, Norway maple, ash and alder. Below you will find a mixture of coppice, bramble and young broadleaves naturally regenerating.

Visitors can enjoy gentle walks using a good network of tracks and rides, which link well with local public rights of way and the adjoining landscape.

Gravetye

East Grinstead

From Turner's Hill, take the B2028 southeast for approximately 1.6km (1 mile). Turn left towards Sharpthorne, and left again into Vowells Lane. Car park is on the right, 400m (0.25 mile)

beyond the entrance to Gravetye Manor. (TQ364351)
257HA (635ACRES)
Forestry Commission

The undulating landscape beneath this large mixed plantation provides contrasting experiences as well as the occasional challenge for visitors.

Where rides are made up the walking is good while other routes have become overgrown and more suitable for the adventurous who have come dressed to explore.

One minute you could be walking beneath huge columns of western hemlock and Corsican pine then through a plantation of beech.

Owned by the William Robinson Charity, named after the gardener credited for the original planting and design of the Gravetye Manor estate, the site is popular with local visitors.

Follow the Sussex Border Path which meanders through the site. Before emerging on the eastern edge, where it continues via the shore of Weir Wood reservoir, you will have experienced the site in all its variety from dense plantation to open areas and a lake.

Friston Forest

Friston

Take the A259 west from Eastbourne. At the Seven Sisters Country Park at Exceat, take the minor road to Litlington on the right. The car park is on the right, 100m beyond the right turn to West Dean village. (TQ519001) 858HA (2,121ACRES) AONB

Forestry Commission

Easy on the eye – and the walker's legs – Friston Forest is developing into a special section of the South Downs Area of Outstanding Natural Beauty.

Colourful in spring and autumn, this plantation is a massive 1920's forest that is dominated by beech. As the trees grow and mature the site will increase in interest. There are occasional large conifers to be seen along the ride edges.

Family visitors are well looked after. Information is available from nearby Seven Sisters Country Park where cycles are available for hire and good picnic facilities are provided near two spacious car parks.

Exploration is along gentle to moderate slopes and waymarked trails cater for cyclists and walkers who can tackle the 1.5-hour White Horse View from the West Dean car park or the slightly shorter one-hour Butchers Trudge route from the Butchershole car park. There is even a Trim Trail for runners – especially devised for the energetic.

Friston

Moat Wood

East Hoathly, Uckfield
South of Uckfield on A22, two
entrances off South Street, East
Hoathly. (TQ516159)
10HA (25ACRES)
The Woodland Trust

A classic example of Sussex
ancient woodland, Moat Wood
is particularly wonderful in
May, with nightingales and
other birds in full song.

Walk into the heart of the
wood and you will discover
a medieval moat, now a scheduled ancient monument,
surrounding a square island of
mixed coppice.

A network of paths and rides
provides access through the
wood, which is emerging as a
real wildlife haven. As rides
can become muddy after rain
the wearing of boots is advised.

Once dominated by a dense
canopy of tall oaks, it was hit
by the storm of 1987. For the
first time in many years areas of
the woodland floor became
open to sunlight. New planting
and natural regeneration has
brought benefits to wildlife.

Bluebells, wood anemone
and an unusual proliferation of
common cow-wheat are clues
to the wood's great age and
there are signs of deer.

Stanmer Great Wood

Brighton
From the A27 east of Brighton, follow
signs for Stanmer Park. The Great
Wood is on the left of the park before
the house. (TQ343087)
60HA (148ACRES) AONB
Brighton and Hove Council

Lying on the slopes to the
south and western edges of
Stanmer Park, the woodland
provides an attractive backdrop
to the busy park below.

Once owned by the Earl of
Chichester, the estate includes a
19th-century manor house (not
open to the public) and park –
the woods have been open to
the public for over 50 years.

The transition from park to
woodland is gradual with plenty
of natural regeneration to
soften the edges. Evidence of
more formal planting can be seen
in wonderful large planes, yew
and cedar (near the house) as
well as the occasional spreading
oak and tall beech. Toward the
northern edge at Chalk Hill
young ash and sycamore are
replacing the mature trees
which fell in the storms of '87.

Main rides link to a maze of
paths winding through the
wood where views can be
glimpsed over the park and
toward the site of Hollingbury
Castle to the south.

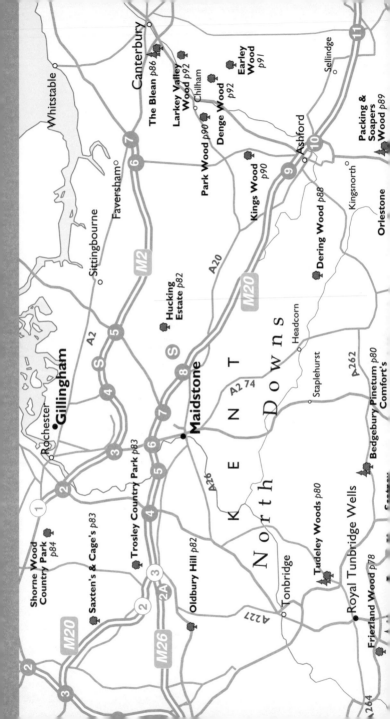

Whitstable

Canterbury

The Blean p86

Larkey Valley Wood p92

Chilham

Earley Wood p91

Sellindge

Denge Wood p92

Park Wood p90

Ashford

Packing & Soapers Wood p89

Kings Wood p90

Faversham

Sittingbourne

Dering Wood p88

Kingsnorth

Orlestone

Hucking Estate p82

A20

K E N T

D o w n s

Headcorn

Staplehurst

Rochester

Gillingham

Trosley Country Park p83

Maidstone

A274

North

A262

Shorne Wood Country Park p84

Saxten's & Cage's p83

Oldbury Hill p82

Tonbridge

Tudeley Woods p80

Bedgebury Pinetum p80
Comfort's

Royal Tunbridge Wells

Friezland Wood p78

264

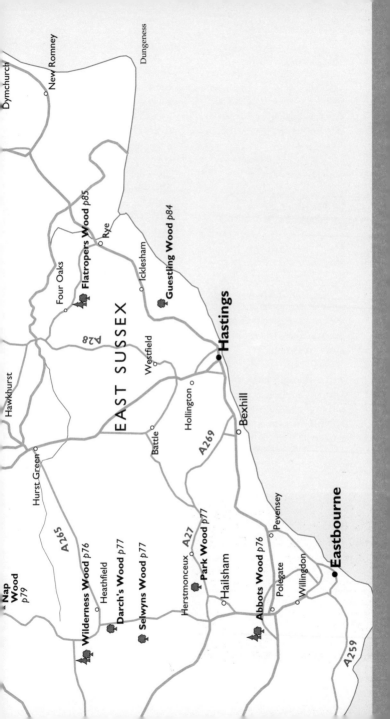

Dymchurch

New Romney

Dungeness

Flatropers Wood *p85*

Rye

Four Oaks

Icklesham

Guestling Wood *p84*

A28

EAST SUSSEX

Westfield

Hastings

Hawkhurst

Hollington

Bexhill

Battle

A269

Hurst Green

A265

Pevensey

A27

Nap Wood *p79*

Wilderness Wood *p76*

Heathfield

Darch's Wood *p77*

Selwyns Wood *p77*

Park Wood *p77*

Herstmonceux

Hailsham

Abbots Wood *p76*

Polegate

Willingdon

Eastbourne

A259

Wilderness Wood

Uckfield

On south side of A272 in Hadlow
Down village, 8km (5 miles) northeast
of Uckfield. Follow brown tourist signs.
(TQ536240)
25HA (61ACRES) AONB
Chris and Anne Yarrow

Hailed for its people-friendly
approach and its commitment
to the environment alike,
Wilderness Wood is a family-
run working woodland that offers
a fully interpreted package –
but still allows you to 'get
away from it all'.

Colourful in spring with wood
anemone and bluebells and
again in autumn with a display
of fungi. Adding atmosphere
are lush mosses, liverworts and
ferns by the stream.

Wilderness Wood

A mile-long woodland trail
allows the visitor to experience
the different habitats. Most of
the woodland, which includes
a small heath, is dominated by
sweet chestnut coppice though
a few mature and ancient trees
survived the 1987 storm. Winter
visitors can cut their own
Christmas trees.

Children are well catered for
and a separate trail is designed
for the less-able.

Abbots Wood

Arlington

Take the A22 south from the Boship
roundabout. Turn right on to minor
road after approx 3km (2 miles), then
take the next left. The car park is on the
left 400m (0.25 mile) beyond The Old
Oak public house. (TQ556074)
356HA (880ACRES)
Forestry Commission

Wonderful spring bluebells are
just one of the seasonal delights
to discover in Abbots Wood.

The site, named during the
reign of Henry I when it was
given to Battle Abbey, has more
ecclesiastical connections – the
lake in its heart was created in
medieval times by monks from
nearby Michelham Priory.

But modern needs are not
forgotten – picnic and
barbecue facilities are

provided, with a children's adventure playground near the car park.

Those keen to explore can choose from two waymarked circular trails. Though these cover a relatively small portion of the site there are other forest tracks and paths to explore on generally level ground.

The wood, which also has some conifer plantations, supports dormice and a range of woodland butterflies – look out for pearl bordered fritillaries.

Park Wood

Hellingly
From A271, travelling east from Upper Horsebridge, turn left into Park Road (signed Hellingly Hospital). Approx 2.5km (1.5 miles) towards Grove Hill car park is on right (TQ603125)
60HA (148ACRES)
East Sussex County Council

Once part of Anderida, an ancient forest that covered vast areas of the southeast, Park Wood has a rich history.

The site once formed part of a medieval deer park – hence the name – and still has signs of ditch and bank system along the boundary. There are also remains of Canadian army trenches from World War II.

Visitors with less interest in historic events can enjoy the atmosphere of this oak-dominated wood where wide and sunny areas contrast with denser, more shaded sections and the walking is not too taxing.

Spring is a good time to enjoy displays of wood anemone, bluebell, yellow archangel and foxgloves while fungi add autumn interest. You might catch a glimpse of roe deer or dormice.

Selwyns Wood

Heathfield or Hailsham
Enter Cross-in-Hand from Heathfield. Take left turn in village into Fir Grove Road. Take track on left marked by Sussex Wildlife Trust sign, next to house called White Lodge (sign tricky to spot). (TQ551205)
11HA (27ACRES) AONB
Sussex Wildlife Trust

Darch's Wood

Heathfield
At Cross-in-Hand turn south into A267 Eastbourne Road. Shortly on right is St Bartholomews Church and car park. Entrance to wood is behind church. (TQ569215)
16HA (40ACRES) AONB
Heathfield and Waldron Parish Council

Eridge Rocks

Tunbridge Wells

Entrance is via a private road off the
A26 in Eridge Green between the
church and a small printing works.
(TQ554355)
40HA (99ACRES) AONB SSSI
Sussex Wildlife Trust

Impressive, even from the car
park, Eridge Rocks supports
ancient, almost gravity-defying
gnarled beech, yew and hollies
which thrive on an ancient
sandstone outcrop dating back
135 million years.

Massive sandstone boulders
stand out among the mixed
woodland and support 150
types of plant – little wonder
this site is designated of special
scientific interest.

There are plans to improve
the already good path network
which meanders through this
quiet and peaceful site.

The woods are a mixture of
chestnut coppice and oak with
a display of bluebells in spring.
Alder trees line the woodland
stream and there is a good
array of birds including tits,
nuthatches and woodpeckers.

The spread of rhododendron,
planted by the Victorians, was
crowding out locally distinctive
plants so Sussex Wildlife Trust
is removing much of it. As a
result, mosses, liverworts and
ferns are now thriving.

Adjoining is Broadwater
Wood, a Scots pine plantation
with beech, birch and oak on
the fringes.

Friezland Wood

Tunbridge Wells

Follow High Rocks Lane east out of
Tunbridge Wells. (TQ562383)
8HA (20ACRES) AONB SSSI
The Woodland Trust

Small but packed with interest,
Friezland Wood on the Kent-
East Sussex border is something
of a British rarity, thanks to the
unusual rock formations on its
western side.

Rising out of the highest
cliffs of the Weald, the Ardingly
Sandstone rock formations are
so unusual they have earned
part of the site SSSI status and
nurtured a rich mixture of
lichens, ferns and bryophytes.

Set on a steep north-facing
slope, the site has three distinct
sections: its upper slopes
feature oak, ash, alder and
birch with an abundance of
wood anemones, bluebells and
some bramble. The vertical
rocks support yew, sessile oak
and holly, with a flatter area
supporting a stand of alder
with buttercups and
celandines.

Popular with local people,

Friezland Wood

Friezland has a good network of paths though some can get muddy and waterlogged in winter.

The remains of a hill fort, dating back to 150–50BC survives a short distance from the southwest boundary of this ancient woodland.

Hargate Forest

Tunbridge Wells
Entrance off Broadwater Down, just off A26. (TQ574370)
61HA (151ACRES) AONB
The Woodland Trust

Set just south of Tunbridge Wells is big, broad and beautiful Hargate Forest – perfect for those 'getting away to the country'.

Part of the heavily wooded High Weald, the mixed wood-land supports an abundance of butterflies not often found in the region and a rich bird population. It is popular with people too!

Hargate has a good track, ride

and path network where you can complete a circular walk but some sections can get muddy.

Set on sloping land, there are extensive views from the regenerating heathland areas and a brook flows through its southern section. The Woodland Trust has created ponds throughout the site.

The old forest, in the south, has the real feel of ancient woodland and boasts some fine old beech trees. Look out for lily of the valley – rare in the region.

Work is ongoing to thin conifers and control rhododendron, encouraging regeneration of native trees and boosting biodiversity.

Nap Wood

Frant
Take the A267 south from Tunbridge Wells. Nap Wood is about 3km (2 miles) south of Frant, on the left opposite a minor road turning to the right. Park on the verge. (TQ583327)
43HA (107ACRES) AONB SSSI
The National Trust

Tudeley Woods

Tonbridge

Take the A21 south from Tonbridge. After 1.6km (1 mile) take minor road to Capel, turning left immediately before Shell garage. Car park is 800m (0.5 mile) on the left. (TQ616433)

287HA (709ACRES)

RSPB

One of the largest areas of ancient woodland in the south-east, Tudeley Woods is a haven for birdlife.

Using traditional techniques such as coppicing and charcoal burning the RSPB is maintaining a thriving wildlife habitat.

This is particularly evident in spring with wonderful shows of bluebells and primroses and the woods are alive with birdsong from a host of warblers breeding here.

The oak woodland supports nuthatches, three woodpecker species and tawny owls while the adjacent meadow is important for willow warblers, whitethroats and yellow hammers and for goldfinches, redpolls and siskins in autumn.

Two waymarked trails take the explorer through areas of light and shade, providing good views over the Kent countryside. Some paths are quite steep and potentially slippery.

Bedgebury Pinetum

Goudhurst

Take the A21 north from Flimwell and after about 1.6km (1 mile) turn right onto the B2079 to Goudhurst. (TQ715388)

120HA (297ACRES) AONB

Forestry Commission

Hailed as one of the world's finest conifer collections, Bedgebury Pinetum boasts a beautiful plantation of 6,000 impressive trees set beside landscaped lakes and valleys.

Located in an Area of Outstanding Natural Beauty, this peaceful scene contains some of Britain's oldest and largest conifers including rare, endangered and historically important trees, around a fabulous lake complete with pretty bridge, beautiful lilies and enchanting reflections.

Founded by the Forestry Commission and Kew Gardens in the 1920s, visitors can enjoy year-round interest: rhododendrons and azaleas in spring; shaded glades, lakes and stream in summer; autumn colour with fungi, fruits and berries and a Christmas card landscape in winter.

Wander at will or take the waymarked 'Trees of the World' trail. Two forest trails in the neighbouring forest incorporate 21 information stops. A programme of educational walks, talks and events ensures adults and children are well catered for.

Scotney Castle Estate

Lamberhurst
2.5km (1.5 miles) south of Lamberhurst, on the east of the A21, 13km (8 miles) southeast of Tunbridge Wells.
(TQ688353)
311HA (770ACRES)
The National Trust

Scotney Castle Estate is beautiful to explore and has a variety of

Scotney

woods to visit.

Stately, old lichen-clad trees dot the open parkland areas. Woodland ranges from ancient trees in Kilndown Wood to mixed broadleaves in High Forest and stands of coppiced sweet chestnut in Collier's Wood.

A garden and shop are open from late March to early November but visitors are advised to check on opening times.

A four-mile waymarked trail leads through mixed woodland – some of it ancient – taking in parkland, meadow and the River Bewl with good views across the estate and parkland to the old ruined castle. Look for oast houses, hop gardens, hoppers' huts and ponds – signs that brewing was once an important part of the local economy.

There are other short, occasionally rough and muddy routes to follow so remember those sturdy boots.

Comfort's Wood

Cranbrook
Take the B2086 from the A229 and head east towards Beneden. Wood is adjacent to Swattenden Lane (B2086) and entrance is opposite the Swattenden Centre. (TQ771346)
11HA (27ACRES) AONB
The Woodland Trust

hornbeam, passing fine examples of mature beech and oak toward new woodland creation schemes. An extensive planting programme, sees 78 hectares of new broadleaved woodland being created.

Clearance work has opened up darker areas, creating wide rides and allowing light to reach the woodland floor, stimulating development of butterfly-attracting flora. Bluebells dominate in spring along with dog's mercury, wood anemone, red campion and foxglove.

Archaeology enthusiasts can examine a host of interesting features, including an ancient drove road, woodbank and marl pits.

Hucking Estate ◘

Hollingbourne
From A20 roundabout near Leeds Castle take B2163 through Hollingbourne towards Sittingbourne. At top of hill at crossroads turn left towards Hucking. After 2.5km (1.5 miles) turn left at junction signed Hucking. Car park 100m on left. (TQ843575)
235HA (581ACRES) AONB
The Woodland Trust

Set in Kent's Downs Area of Outstanding Natural Beauty, the Hucking Estate is a mix of farmland and woods with a wealth of archaeological 'gems'.

A series of paths, including two waymarked trails, guide visitors through areas of coppiced ash, sweet chestnut, sycamore and

Oldbury Hill ◘

Sevenoaks
On the north side of the A25, 5km (3 miles) southwest of Wrotham. (TQ582561)
62HA (153ACRES) AONB SSSI
The National Trust

Stepping into the woodland of Oldbury Hill is like stepping back in history.

This is the site of an Iron Age fortress with massive ramparts – one of them is a mammoth 4km (2.5 miles) long. Built in

100–50BC by the Wealden Celts, it is one of our largest hillforts whose gateways controlled an important crossing of the River Medway.

As you walk beneath the huge beeches that grow on the ramparts today or along the route of the prehistoric track that crosses the site – it is not difficult to conjure up characters from the past.

Parts of the mixed woodland – oak, birch, rowan, beech and some Scots pine – has probably been coppiced since Saxon times.

Visitors can view the site from two steep waymarked trails taking in the dappled shade of open woodland.

Trosley Country Park

Meopham
From the A227 follow signs to Vigo Village. Turn right into Waterlow Road and park is opposite. (TQ634612)
69HA (170ACRES)
Kent County Council

Natural without being wild and well laid out without being over-interpreted, Trosley Country Park on the crest of the North Downs is a great place to explore.

Two main routes serve the woodland, which boast a wonderful bluebell display in the spring and provides fantastic views across the Weald. The red route runs via a long straight path cut into the side of the hill, where overhanging trees create a striking tunnel effect. En route are seats and sculptures and some large, impressive yew trees.

The blue route is a steep hilly path across chalk downland where Exmoor ponies graze and the spring and summer show of wildflowers adds colour.

Wildlife thrives here with red admiral, speckled wood and common blues among the butterfly population. Rare species such as the chalkhill blue and green fritillary live on the chalk grassland. Birds include woodpecker, kestrel, hawfinch and treecreeper.

Saxten's & Cage's

Fawkham Green
From Farningham take A20 towards West Kingsdown and after 2.5km (1.5 miles) turn left, signposted Fawkham Green. Opposite Brands Hatch circuit turn left for Fawkham Green going underneath M20 and turn right immediately into Roger's Wood Lane. Continue up a short hill, main entrance on left at the top of hill. (TQ586649)
23HA (57ACRES) AONB
The Woodland Trust

Shorne Wood Country Park

Shorne

Adjacent to the A2, between Gravesend
and Rochester. Take Shorne/Cobham
turning. Country Park is signposted
from A2 with brown signs. (TQ684699)
70HA (174ACRES) SSSI
Kent County Council

There is plenty to keep visitors
happy – delightful ancient
woodland, heathland, wetland,
meadows, a 3-km horse and
cycle route, fishing lake,
sensory garden and even a dog
swimming pond!

There is a real country park
feel to the area surrounding the
car park and visitor centre so
many people might never be
tempted to stray far. There is a
busy events programme,
children's adventure playground
and a 'Wood Henge' seating
feature as well as a range of
woodland sculptures carved
from fallen chestnut. An excellent
arboretum in the centre of the
car park is planted with clearly
labelled native trees – excellent
for woodland 'novices'.

Follow the purple or red trails
to discover 'real' woodland
with some large trees,
including birch, sweet chestnut,
oak, sycamore and beech.

Guestling Wood

Hastings

Car park situated in Watermill Lane
between Pett and Icklesham.
(TQ861147)
21HA (52ACRES) AONB
The Woodland Trust

Spring brings the promise of
spectacular wood anemone and
bluebell displays in Guestling
Wood, a typical High Weald
ancient woodland.

The Woodland Trust owns
around half of the sweet chestnut-
dominated site. Guestling's
rich ground flora is being
encouraged through a programme
of coppicing, particularly in
the northern part of the wood.

Two public footpaths and a
good network of rides and
paths link the site with
surrounding countryside and
lead the visitor through
frequent scene changes.

The eastern side sits on top
of a ridge which falls away to
the west. A small stream, known
as Lady Brook, flows along the
site's western boundary.

In contrast, the lower section
of the wood is much wetter,
with different ground and tree
cover. Edging the stream are
willow, alder and ash with
clumps of sedge and rush at
their base. Further south, the
chestnut makes way for hazel

Guestling

coppice while oak standards dot the entire site.

Flatropers Wood

Rye

Entrance on east side of Bixley Lane, which leaves A268 on south side of a sharp bend south of Beckley. (Bixley Lane becomes unsurfaced a short distance from A268.) (TQ861231) 35HA (87ACRES) AONB
Sussex Wildlife Trust

Birdsong is all that is likely to break the peace on a walk through remote Flatropers Wood, a mixed woodland in a quiet corner of Sussex.

Although surrounded by conifer plantations, the unspoilt mixture of oak, horn-beam, hazel and occasional pine plantation provides a delightful variety of wildlife habitats.

It takes between one and two hours to tour the reserve over generally gentle terrain that can get muddy underfoot in winter.

Inside the wood are areas of large oaks, cleared birch areas where heather and other heathland plants support lizards and insects such as the rare green tiger beetle.

Coppicing has created sunny spots where spring flowers burst into life, supporting a variety of butterflies. Interest is added by a stream and small pond on the eastern side of the wood.

Wild boar hoof prints are occasionally spotted on the paths, though the animals themselves are a much rarer sight.

Hemsted Forest

Cranbrook

From the crossroads at the west end of Benenden village, turn north towards Sissinghurst. Take the next right oppo-site the entrance to Benenden School. The car park is on the left after about 400m (0.25 mile). (TQ812345) 397HA (981ACRES) AONB
Forestry Commission

Blean Wood

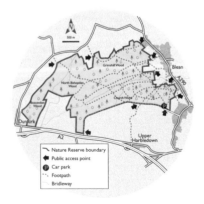

Canterbury

Situated between the A2 and A290. From A2 take exit signposted Canterbury and left signposted Rough Common. At north end of Rough Common, small brown sign on left indicates Blean NNR. Follow stoned track into wood to car park, 300 metres. (TR102593) 530HA (1310 ACRES) SSSI

Various

The Blean, Kent's second most extensive concentration of woodland, is one of the largest broadleaved nature reserves in Britain. The Woodland Trust, English Nature and the RSPB manage the Blean National Nature Reserve (NNR) as a partnership.

The Blean makes up the northwestern half of a great ring of woods surrounding Canterbury. Despite its vast size visitors still find these woods intimate and constant habitat changes keep your interest alive.

The area is managed to protect its valuable mosaic of habitats which vary from sunny glades and heathland to ancient woodland, areas of coppice and conifer plantation, much of which is being thinned and nurtured back to native broadleaves.

Easy enough to reach from minor roads and tracks, the woodlands of the Blean remain relatively remote though they have seen many changes over the centuries.

The area's mature woodland boasts some large oak with, less frequently, beech and decaying trees that help sustain a vast array of wildlife. Some 29 species of butterfly have been recorded here as well as an impressive number of woodland birds, dormice and even ants which thrive in huge wood nests.

In spring some of the woods are positively idyllic, with fine floral displays of bluebell, wood anemone, primrose, violet and ladies smock edging the paths.

From the car park, four colour-coded waymarked trails range from just a mile to more than seven. Dog owners have their own route. And there are many other rides and tracks to explore. Generally flat, they vary in shape and size from meandering path to wide forest tracks. Growing along some rides is the less-than-common, common cow wheat, an essential food plant for the rare heath fritillary butterfly.

Close to the car park is a picnic area with interactive sculptures – a man-made addition to the Blean's more natural features.

Dering Wood

Pluckley

From A20 at Charing take road signposted Pluckley and Smarden. 400m (0.25 mile) after Pluckley turn right on road beside pub. After 2.5km (1.5 miles) the road passes between woodland. Dering Wood car park is on the left. (TQ900441)

125HA (310ACRES)

The Woodland Trust

Saved from development, Dering Wood can now continue to support its vast array of plant and wildlife that is recognised for its conservation interest.

The wood is home to more than 25 species of butterfly and rare beetles and renowned for its stunning display of spring bluebells and wood anemones.

Mostly ancient woodland, the site features in records stretching back 1,000 years. Archaeological evidence can be spotted in the shape of drainage ditches, ponds, saw pits and even the site of a plane crash.

Oak and hornbeam coppice covers much of Dering, a distinctive feature of the south-east. While there are areas of high forest and dense scrubby woodland, mature coppice dominates.

Typical of Weald woodlands, underfoot can get very wet and muddy in winter but is well served with access tracks.

Dering Wood

Packing & Soapers Wood

Hamstreet

Situated 1.6km (1 mile) north of Hamstreet on the west of A2070 bypass. However, access is not advised off the A2070. Take road through Hamstreet heading north towards Bromley Green. After A2070 turning take second right at staggered crossroads into Capel Lane. Entrance on right after approximately 1km (0.75 mile). (TR005352)
41HA (101ACRES) SSSI
The Woodland Trust

Hamstreet Woods

Ashford, Kent

Turn off A2070 Ashford to Brenzett road into centre of Hamstreet. Follow one way system at crossroads to Dukes Head PH. Turn left at pillarbox just before Bournewood Stores. Continue to end of this no-through road to car park and main entrance. (TR011341)
97HA (240ACRES) SSSI
English Nature

Hamstreet Woods, the 'star' site among a large complex of woods descended from a post-Ice Age forest, is nationally renowned for birds and moths.

Rare moths with such descriptive names as silky wave, merveille-du-jour, light orange underwing and the triangle populate this traditionally managed site. The site is of interest from first shoots of spring to the autumn when it is swathed in rich colour.

More than 30 species of trees and shrubs are found here. Oak and hornbeam thrive alongside wood anemones, bluebells and the occasional wild service tree in higher parts of the wood. In the damp valleys you'll discover ash, hazel and alder rising from a woodland floor covered with dog's mercury and orchids such as the greater butterfly and early purple.

Sited on the edge of a sandstone and clay plateau and sliced by a number of small valleys, the site can be explored by following three waymarked trails of varying lengths.

Orlestone Forest

Ashford

From Ham Street village take A2070 towards Ashford. After 2.5km (1.5 miles), at the next crossroads, turn left and left again. The car park is on the right, 50m beyond this junction. (TQ986348)
451HA (1,115ACRES) SSSI
Forestry Commission

Park Wood

Chilham
2.5km (1.5 miles) southwest of
Chilham, adjacent to A252. (TR042526)
23HA (57ACRES) AONB SSSI
The Woodland Trust

Visitors to this ancient woodland can enjoy a wood of two
distinctive halves.

On the western side you can
stroll beneath a mixed canopy of
fine old sweet chestnuts and oaks
with coppiced hornbeam beneath.
By contrast, to the east of the main
gateway is a more dense cover
including hazel and hawthorn.

Within the coppiced areas
there are also many old
pollarded hornbeam trees.
These were frequently used by
woodcutters to mark the
boundary of coppiced areas.

The site can be explored via
two good circular paths which
lead through the wood from
inside the main gateway. The
paths are edged with a wonderful
collection of flowering plants
which are particularly good for
butterflies. To maintain this
important habitat, the Trust
regularly coppices edges of the
path network.

While the ground is gently
undulating there are short
sections which can be steep and
slippery in winter.

Kings Wood

Ashford
Take the A28 to Canterbury from
Ashford. Approx 5km (3 miles) out of
Ashford turn left towards Challock.
Car park is 2.5km (1.5 miles) on the
right. (TR025500)
574HA (1419ACRES) AONB
Forestry Commission

Autumn is one of the best
times to visit, when Kings
Wood is full of colour and
sweet chestnuts can be
harvested.

The woods are best viewed
by taking the Beech Walk, a
three-mile trail, where children
can delight in discovering
sculptures created by local artists.

Varied paths lead visitors
through closed canopies and
open spaces. As well as
conifers, which are the
dominant feature, pockets of
ancient woodland survive with
yew and hornbeam and
coppiced areas of beech as well
as sweet chestnut.

Bluebell and lady orchid are
among the many beautiful
floral species that thrive here.
Bird sightings include
goldcrest, nightingale and three
species of woodpecker.

Close to the car park is a
picnic area with play sculptures
while older visitors appreciate
views from the open area nearby.

Earley Wood

Petham
Situated between Petham and Waltham.
From Petham village take road southwest signposted Waltham. After about
1km (0.75 mile) Earley Wood and car
park spaces are on the left. (TR120502)
22HA (54ACRES) AONB
The Woodland Trust

Mystery surrounds the origins
of Earley Wood, but the heart
of the site is thought to be
ancient woodland.

The wood forms part of the
North Kent Downs Area of
Outstanding Natural Beauty
and offers views over countryside to the south.

It is a rich mix of coppiced
broadleaved woodland with
oak, ash, beech, chestnut and
occasional sycamore.

A splendid beech and
hornbeam avenue that used to
stand in the heart of the wood
was damaged in the 1987
storm.

Around 110 different plant
species, including many small
colonies of herb paris, a
wonderful collection of orchids
and swathes of bluebells, clothe
the woodland floor in spring.

Badgers and birds thrive on
the site with dark bush crickets
and speckled bush crickets
being two of the many rare
invertebrates recorded here.
Watch out, too, for adders in
the area formerly called
Deadley's Wood.

Earley Wood

Denge Wood

Garlinge Green, Chartham

From A28 turn off to Shalmsford Street and, reaching the eastern end of the village, turn right into Mystole Lane and right again after approximately 1km (0.75 mile) into Penny Pot Lane. After 1.6km (1 mile) the road enters Denge Wood with car parking space on the left. (TR104523)

26HA (64ACRES) AONB

The Woodland Trust

Larkey Valley Wood

Canterbury

Take A28 from Canterbury towards Ashford and first left into St Nicholas Road after crossing over A2 and follow road round to right into Cockering

Denge Wood

Road. Car park is 1.6km (1 mile) on the left. (TR124557)

43HA (106ACRES) SSSI

Canterbury City Council

Spring is probably the best time to enjoy Larkey Valley Wood, when it is filled with a mass of flowers, the star of which is the rare lady orchid, one of eight orchid species growing here.

This is an ancient woodland site, with a wide variety of trees and shrubs. To identify the soil under your feet look for beech and hazel which grow on chalky soil while oak, hornbeam and sweet chestnut enjoy areas of more acidic clay with flints.

There is an extensive path network and two waymarked routes. Paths can be narrow and slippery in the wet.

The storm of 1987 has left its mark with dense thickets taking over parts of the south and eastern edge though some clearance work has been undertaken. The traditional practice of coppicing can still be seen in parts of the wood.

From the car park, views extend over the Great Stour valley and surrounding countryside.

Further Information

The Woodland Trust

Registered Charity No 294344. The Woodland Trust logo is a registered trademark.

Trees and forests are crucial to life on our planet. They generate oxygen, play host to a spectacular variety of wildlife and provide us with raw materials and shelter. They offer us tranquillity, inspire us and refresh our souls.

Founded in 1972, the Woodland Trust is now the UK's leading woodland conservation charity. By acquiring sites and campaigning for woodland it aims to conserve, restore and re-establish native woodland to its former glory. The Trust now owns and cares for over 1,100 woods throughout the UK.

The Woodland Trust wants to see:

* no further loss of ancient woodland
* the variety of woodland wildlife restored and improved
* an increase in new native woodland
* an increase in people's awareness and enjoyment of woodland

The Woodland Trust has over 120,000 members who share this vision. It only costs £2.50 a month to join but your support would be of great help in ensuring the survival of Britain's magnificent woodland heritage. For every new member, the Trust can care for approximately half an acre of native woodland. For details of how to join the Woodland Trust please either ring FREEPHONE 0800 026 9650 or visit the website at www.woodland-trust.org.uk

If you have enjoyed the woods in this book please consider leaving a legacy to the Woodland Trust. Legacies of all sizes play an invaluable role in helping the Trust to create new woodland and secure precious ancient woodland threatened by development and destruction. For further information please either call 01476 581129 or visit our dedicated website at www.legacies.org.uk

Public transport

Each entry gives a brief description of location, nearest town and grid reference. Traveline provides impartial journey planning information about all public transport services either by ringing 0870 608 2608 (calls charged at national rates) or visit www.traveline.org.uk. For information about the Sustrans National Cycle Network either ring 0117 929 0888 or visit www.sustrans.org.uk

Useful contacts

Forestry Commission, 0845 367 3787, www.forestry.gov.uk
National Trust, 0870 458 4000, www.nationaltrust.org.uk
Wildlife Trusts, 0870 036 7711, www.wildlifetrusts.org
RSPB, 01767 680551, www.rspb.org.uk
Royal Forestry Society, 01442 822028, www.rfs.org.uk
National Community Forest Partnership, 01684 311880, www.communityforest.org.uk
Woodland Trust, 01476 581111, www.woodland-trust.org.uk

Index

Legal & General is delighted to support the Woodland Trust's conservation programme across the UK.

As a leading UK company, Legal & General recognises the importance of maintaining and improving our environment for future generations. We actively demonstrate our commitment through good management and support of environmental initiatives and organisations, such as the Woodland Trust.

Information on how Legal & General manages its impact on the environment can be found at www.legalandgeneral.com/csr.